Surveying adoption

A comprehensive analysis of local authority adoptions 1998/99 – England

BAAF Adoption
Statistics Project

Written by
Gilles Ivaldi

British
Agencies
for **A**doption
and **F**ostering

Published by
British Agencies for Adoption & Fostering
(BAAF)
Skyline House
200 Union Street
London SE1 0LX

Registered charity 275689

© BAAF 2000

British Library Cataloguing in Publication Data
A catalogue record for this book is available
from the British Library

ISBN 1 873868 96 0

Designed by Andrew Haig & Associates
Typeset by Avon Dataset Ltd, Bidford on Avon,
Warwickshire B50 4JH
(www.avondataset.com)
Printed by PIMS (UK) Ltd

Contents

Acknowledgements

This study is the fourth publication of BAAF's Adoption Statistics Project. The Project is supported by the Department of Health with whom BAAF has worked in close collaboration since the early stages of the research. Co-operation with the present study was recommended by the Association of Directors of Social Services (ADSS) and the study has benefited from the support and advice of all the members of BAAF's Adoption Statistics Project Steering Group.

Felicity Collier, Chief Executive, BAAF
Deborah Cullen, Legal Group Secretary, BAAF
Marcus Carlton, Statistician, Children's Statistics Division, Department of Health
Mike Cornish, Statistician, Children's Statistics Division, Department of Health
Jim Cullen, Director, Catholic Caring Services
Cherilyn Dance, Research Co-ordinator, Institute of Psychiatry, London
Mary Gandy, Director, Catholic Child Welfare Council
Julia Ridgway, Inspector, Adoption Policy, Social Services Inspectorate, Department of Health
Anne Van-Meeuwen, Principal Policy and Practice Officer, Barnado's

Our thanks are due to all participating local authorities which completed and returned the present survey. We are indebted to them both for their time and the additional comments and suggestions many of them made in the preparatory phase of the research.

We wish to express our gratitude to Gael Wright, Research Assistant at BAAF, and David Harris, who carried out the difficult task of computerising the impressive amount of data collected from the participating agencies.

We are especially grateful to Mike Cornish and Marcus Carlton from the Department of Health Children's Statistics Division for the help we received in deriving the appropriate grossing up factors for the sample in the present study, and for providing the relevant background information concerning children looked after by local authorities in England.

Special thanks are also due to the contribution of voluntary adoption agencies for their help throughout this project.

Finally, we would like to thank the Hilden Charitable Fund for their contribution towards the project.

Background to the study

While there has been a considerable amount of adoption research at the level of small-scale qualitative studies, there is a distinct dearth of analyses employing a quantitative framework to provide baseline information about looked after children who join new adoptive families. Much emphasis has been placed on the enormous changes in the pattern of adoption over the past decades (Fratter *et al*, 1991), but little research has attempted to supply the statistical data needed to assess both the relevance and the extent of the changes that have occurred in adoption patterns since the late 1960s.

Since the Children Act 1989 was implemented in 1991, the sociological change in adoption has been accompanied by concern as to whether the current legal framework gives sufficient emphasis to the child's need for permanence and stability. In 1996 the Draft Adoption Bill, *Adoption – A Service for Children* (Department of Health, 1996), highlighted the importance of bringing adoption law in line with the principles in the Children Act, including making the child's welfare the court's and agencies' paramount consideration. This view is also echoed by the Adoption Law Reform Group (2000, p.1):

> *Adoption law should provide a more child-centred framework, making the child's welfare the paramount consideration, making the child a party to adoption proceedings, and imposing on courts and agencies, child-centred general duties imposed by the Children Act 1989 in other forms of placement.*

Critical issues such as placement for minority ethnic children, adoption for older children, the growing number of children with special difficulties, and placement for groups of siblings have been well documented by child care and adoption research (Reich and Batty, 1990; Murch and Lowe, 1993; Triseliotis *et al*, 1997; Parker, 1999).

At the same time, adoption has attracted much public attention and is still a matter of debate. In spite of all the efforts that have been made to address these important issues in a "scientific" and non-controversial manner, growing concerns with the careers of children in the public care system and the poor outcomes they experience on leaving care have led to substantial criticisms of local authority and adoption agency practice, sometimes based on the evidence of inspections but, at other times, on an enduring mythology which owes much to the media for its creation.

In recent years, significant improvements have been made by central government bodies in the process of collecting routine statistical information from all adoption agencies throughout the country. There has been an increasing awareness of the need for more reliable and accurate data concerning adopted children, not only to dispel some of the myths in adoption but also to provide the necessary statistical benchmarks to inform both practice and policy-making. As indicated by Parker (1999, p.108), a particularly important aspect of adoption and child care practice by social services departments is the provision of accurate information:

> *One objective of adoption policy must be the encouragement of the collection, in as standardised and discriminating form as possible, of those statistical data which are needed to improve the quality of key decisions at all levels of the adoption service.*

Changes in practice are also likely to have resulted from the 1998 Local Authority Circular *Adoption: Achieving the Right Balance* and the large-scale survey of social services departments that was associated with the implementation of the Circular. The survey demonstrated the need for greater compliance with the circular and better statistical data. In July 2000, *The Prime Minister's Review of Adoption*, issued for consultation by The Performance and Innovation Unit, has similarly pointed to the lack of reliable data on agency adoptions.

In spite, however, of these many real changes, which should lead to improved data being available in the future, there remains little information available at a national level to inform the changes in practice now required. There continues to be a striking contrast between media coverage and publicity surrounding adoption practice by social services departments, on the one hand, and the evident paucity of data on the other. Information about many of the critical issues which are at stake in the public debate about adoption is currently absent in the central government publications (Fruin, 1980, pp.25–36; Evandrou, 1991, p.1; SSI, 1996b; Triseliotis *et al*, 1997, p.15; Dance, 1997, pp.7–9).

There is still room for studies that would aim to draw a more comprehensive picture of the characteristics and experiences of the children leaving the public care system for adoption.

1.1 Adoption for looked after children: a background picture

Published figures for adoption out of care are based on the data collected for the purpose of monitoring numbers of children in the public care system. The *Children Looked After by Local Authorities* annual publication, which represented until recently the only source of statistical information concerning adoption for looked after children in England, is normally used, among other purposes, for the evaluation of the outcome of policy initiatives and the monitoring of trends by the Department of Health (DoH) and the Social Services Inspectorate (SSI).

In recent years, efforts have been made to remedy the deficit of statistical information about adoption by further exploiting the data routinely collected from local authorities. Details of adoption statistics currently made available to the public by the DoH are summarised in Table 1.1 below.

Table 1.1

Adoption of looked after children (1994–1999) – England

Note: Looked after children adopted during the years ending 31 March 1994 to 1999 – Source: Department of Health, *Children Looked After by Local Authorities* – Year Ending 31 March 1999 England, A/F 99/12, Personal Social Services, Local Authority Statistics, 2000.

	1994	1995	1996	1997	1998	1999
All children (N)	2,300	2,100	1,900	1,900	2,100	2,200
Gender						
% of boys	51	50	51	50	51	48
Age at adoption						
% under 1 year	9	10	8	8	7	9
% 1 to 4 years	40	40	45	48	53	57
% 5 to 9 years	34	34	32	31	31	26
% 10 years and over	17	16	15	14	9	7
Legal status at adoption						
% freed for adoption	21	26	30	31	33	33
% care order	57	52	50	51	51	47
% voluntary agreement (S20)	22	23	20	18	16	20

The total number of children adopted from care fell from 2,300 in 1994 to 1,900 in 1997, then rose again from 2,000 in 1998 to 2,200 in the financial year ending March 1999.*

With regard to the characteristics of the children adopted from the care of local authorities, the figures published by the DoH allow examination of gender, age and legal status at adoption. As can be seen from Table 1.1, the proportion of children aged 5 years and over at adoption has been falling gradually since 1994, with a mean age of 5 years 11 months in that year compared to 4 years 11 months in 1998, and 4 years 4 months in 1999. This trend coincides with a reduction in the age of children entering care (see Chapter 3). The above figures also suggest that the use of freeing orders has been increasing over the 1994–99 period of time and was used for a third of the children adopted during 1998/99 as opposed to a fifth in the financial year ending March 1994.

Apart from this fairly basic information, the adoption statistics published by the DoH contain no information with regard to some of the most salient issues in relation to adoption for looked after children. As acknowledged by LAC (98)20:

> *Poor quality aggregated information clearly impacts on some Social Services Departments' planning of their adoption services and recruitment for future needs. It also raises doubts about how they can monitor effectively progress in the lives of an individual child at a senior and departmental level.*

1.2   Issues in adoption out of care

Crucial to the purpose of this introductory chapter is a reminder to the reader of some of the key features of the changing adoption patterns, and why those features can be relevant to the analysis of adoption work by local authorities. These critical issues are examined in turn in the following sections. The aims of the study will be explained in Chapter 2.

1.2.1   The changing profile of children

The late 1970s saw a sharp decline in the number of young babies relinquished for adoption. This downward trend was accompanied by a significant change in the concept of "adoptability" and an increasing interest in the possibility of adoption for large numbers of children previously thought to be "unadoptable" such as older children, those with special needs, sibling groups or black children, including those of mixed parentage.

As early as 1973, the research project *Children who Wait* (Rowe and Lambert, 1973) had shown that a significant number of children in care were in need of permanent family placement and had already spent much of their childhood in public care.

Over the years, patterns of adoption have thus fundamentally changed from being primarily a service to provide babies for childless couples to a more child-focused response to the need of some children for permanent new families (Reich and Batty, 1990, p.6).

---

* Analysis of local authority aggregate data collected in 1999 for the purpose of the *Performance Assessment Framework* (PAF) revealed a wide variation in the numbers of children leaving care through adoption. On average, local authorities had arranged adoption for about 15 of their looked after children during 1998/99, with a range from no adoptions in some agencies to about 70 in some other authorities (standard deviation was 13). See Department of Health, *Personal Social Services Performance Assessment Framework* (PSS/PAF), 1998/99. The Performance Assessment System (PAF) for social services builds on and supports the wider Best Value arrangements across local government. The system aims to bring together all the information about the performance of each local social services authority.

As indicated by Lowe and Murch (1999, p.8) in their recent study of adoption of older children:

Adoption of older children previously looked after by local authorities is a significant aspect of current adoption practice. In contrast to the traditional model of baby adoption, which has markedly declined (...), the proportion of older children being adopted from care in accordance with childcare policies based on so-called "permanency planning" has steadily increased.

In many other respects, the characteristics of the children needing placement can be regarded as very different from those of the infants adopted 30 years ago. The depth of this change in the profile of children adopted from the care of local authorities was, for example, acknowledged by the SSI (1999, p.3) in the introduction to the report, *Meeting the Challenges of Changes in Adoption*, together with the need for extensive partnership between statutory and voluntary adoption agencies:

The volume of work with parents considering adoption for their infant has reduced greatly (...) The majority of children needing placement now being referred to Voluntary Adoption Agencies by Social Services Departments are older, have more complex care histories and often present challenging behaviour. They are likely to have established relationships with birth families or previous caregivers, to be part of sibling groups or have other special needs making them harder for the SSD to place within its own resources.

The children who were previously considered "hard-to-place" include those with a background of abuse or neglect, special needs, learning or physical disabilities, and those needing therapeutic support. Behavioural problems of various kinds are associated with a risk of disruption and adoption breakdown. Defiant, aggressive or sexualised behaviours are also indicators of risk in several of the studies (Parker, 1999, p.16).

One of the most significant challenges to contemporary adoption practice is the placement of groups of birth siblings together. The Children Act stresses the general importance of continuity in family relationships and includes siblings within this. Yet previous research has demonstrated that the possibility of achieving this continuity can vary enormously. As shown by Ellison (1999, p.132), 66 per cent of children with a current plan involving adoption were separated from some or all of their siblings.

"Race" and ethnicity

"Race" and ethnicity as variables in adoption have been largely ignored in terms of the collection of national data, irrespective of the fact that adoption has always fascinated researchers and there are volumes of research on adoption generally (Hill and Shaw, 1998, p.195).

There is (...) very little research on transracial adoption in the United Kingdom. We do not know how many black children are in care, what proportion are fostered or adopted, nor the proportion that are placed in transracial settings. We do not know the outcomes of children beyond teenage years who were transracially adopted.

The issue that has recently attracted most attention with respect to local authority policies is what has come to be referred to as "same-race placement". As explained by Parker (1999, pp.115–116):

Although there appears to be a widespread acceptance in the regulations and guidance that children are best placed with families whose ethnicity and culture resemble their own, disagreement persists about how this is to be interpreted and about what grounds there might be for exceptions to be made. The difficulty of interpretation arises from the large number of variations that there can be in both a child's ethnic and cultural heritage and in that of prospective adopters.

Various statistics are quoted to indicate the importance of same race adoption and the occurrence of transracial adoption – they vary from 50 per cent of all adoptions of minority ethnic children in an SSI Inspection of six local authorities (1996a) to 24 per cent in BAAF's study of 48 local authorities (Dance, 1997). In the *Prime Minister's Review of Adoption* (2000) concerns are highlighted about delay in placement and the shortage of adopters from minority ethnic backgrounds. Accurate information about the ethnicity of children and their adopters is vital to inform policy development – this has been hampered by the lack of ethnic monitoring in the looked after children's statistics, although this has been introduced with effect from April 2000.

1.2.2 Birth families

While the social and demographics factors of children in care have been well documented by research, there has been relatively little attempt to investigate the background history and social and demographic characteristics of birth families whose children are adopted through local authority care. It is generally believed that very young single mothers are over-represented and that birth parents are generally in the lowest income groups. In view of the changing profile of children put forward for adoption by local authorities, there are a number of factors concerning the birth families of the children which may influence future adoption policy and also the provision of support to these families.

Older children leaving care for the purpose of adoption are more likely to have developed relationships with their birth parents and siblings, and the value of more open adoption and adoption with contact for many of these children is widely recognised.

1.2.3 The profile of adopters

The enormous changes in the pattern of adoption has encouraged new thinking about which children are eligible for adoption and who is eligible to adopt.

It is important to understand better the profile of those families or individuals who apply to adopt looked after children, in particular their ages, marital status, and ethnicity. It is also important to look at the actual composition of the adoptive family household, the presence or not of older children, the child's position in the family and the age gaps between children (Triseliotis *et al*, 1997, p.218).

As explained by Parker (1999, p.16):

Many of the children are placed in already established families where other children are to be taken into account. Virtually all the studies found that the presence of birth children increased the risk of poorer outcomes. Some, however, reported that the age differences mattered whilst others did not.

Given the importance attached to reducing looked after children's moves in care, with consequent breaks in attachment, another important issue is the level of involvement of previous foster carers, and their contribution to adoption for looked after children. This would allow for more consideration to be given to whether there is scope for more adoptions by foster carers.

1.2.4   The length of proceedings in agency adoptions

Previous child care research has drawn attention to the importance of considering adoption as a continuing process, and not a single discrete event. The *Pathways to Adoption* report (Murch and Lowe, 1993) identified several stages in the adoption process. First, for some children who were placed initially on the basis of foster care there was the period between that placement and the panel's approval of it for adoption. The second stage in the process was that between the panel approval of the placement for adoption and the submission of an application to court. Taking into account the stages between the application to the court and the granting of an adoption order, the Pathways research found that 12 per cent of the cases had been completed in under three months; 52 per cent within six months, and another 17 per cent between six months and a year. This was based on a sample of all applications, including step-parent adoptions, but does relate to a period in the late 1980s.

Delays which children may encounter during their time in care are currently among the major areas of concern and criticism. LAC (98)20 highlights a number of issues in planning for individual children and states:

> *Planning should be timely and should recognise when attempts at reunification with the birth family should cease. Having made plans these should be implemented without delay and, where possible, contingency arrangements should be made to reduce the time children spend in care before joining their permanent families.*

Similarly, the *Prime Minister's Review of Adoption* (2000) recommends:

> *. . . setting time-scales and performance indicators to improve performance and avoid damaging drift and delay for children.*

Furthermore, it is essential to assess the potential impact of the child's characteristics, needs and early experiences on the subsequent development of adoption proceedings. There may be significant differences in duration of care when considering the profile, needs and family history of the children. As explained, for example, by the recent review of the Children Act 1989 Cm4579 (2000, p.31) with regard to the influence of legal proceedings:

> *The time it takes to secure adoptions for looked after children (...)varies very significantly with the legal status of the child which, in turn, probably reflects the complexity of children's circumstances.*

1.2.5   Partnerships between local authorities and voluntary adoption agencies

The implementation of the Adoption Act 1976 required reorganisation and adaptation for both local authorities and voluntary agencies. Local authorities had been empowered to function as adoption agencies by the Adoption Act 1958 but the adoption provisions of the Children Act 1975 (consolidated in the 1976 Act), in accordance with the recommendations of the Houghton Committee specifically required all authorities to ensure that a comprehensive adoption service was available in their area (Cmnd5107, 1972; SSI, DoH, 1997).

The provision of a comprehensive adoption service required co-operation between local authorities and voluntary adoption agencies within their area. Successive reports have attested to the important contribution made by the voluntary adoption sector and the particular skills and expertise which voluntary agencies have achieved in adoption practice.

It is generally believed that many local authorities do not place children with voluntary adoption agencies, or indeed with families provided by other local authorities, because of the cost of the "inter-agency fee" (a levy charged generally at an agreed national rate, to offset the recruitment and support costs incurred by the family's agency). It is therefore of considerable interest to ascertain how many placements are made on an inter-agency basis and whether they are more common for particular groups of children.

There are indications of the value of consortia and other forms of collaboration between the voluntary and the statutory sectors, and it is therefore important to draw a more accurate picture of the extent of co-operation between adoption agencies throughout the country. Some progress towards a more uniform and consistent adoption service seems to have been made through various schemes of inter-agency collaboration. As stated by Parker (1999, p.120):

> *Policies which encourage the participation of agencies in regional consortia, or in co-ordinated national activities are likely to create more consistency in the services as well as more opportunities for sharing of all kinds and the cutting of certain costs (...) Consistency (it may be called standardisation, rationalisation, coherence or uniformity) has to be accorded a prominent place on the national and local policy agendas, the more so now if the objectives of the Quality Protects programme are to be realised and if ideas about the establishment of national standards are to be applied.*

References

Adoption Law Reform Group (2000) *Reforming Adoption Law in England and Wales*, London: BAAF.

Cm 4579 (2000) *The Children Act Report 1995 – 1999*, London: The Stationery Office.

Dance, C (1997) *Focus on Adoption: A snapshot of adoption patterns in England – 1995*, London: BAAF.

Department of Health (1996) *Adoption – A Service for Children*, London: HMSO.

Department of Health (1998) *Adoption: Achieving the Right Balance*, LAC (98)20, London: Department of Health.

Ellison, M (1999) 'Needs Led or Needs Unmet', in Mullender, A (ed.) *We are Family: Sibling relationships in placement and beyond*, London: BAAF.

Evandrou, M (ed.) (1991) *Improving Government Statistics*, Social Science Forum.

Fratter, J Rowe, J Sapsford, D and Thoburn, J (1991) *Permanent Family Placement: A decade of experience*, London: BAAF.

Fruin, D (1980) 'Sources of Statistical Information on Adoption', *Adoption & Fostering*, 100 (2).

Hill, M and Shaw, M (1998) *Signposts in Adoption: Policy, practice and research*, London: BAAF.

Houghton Report (1972) *Report of the Departmental Committee on the Adoption of Children*, Cmnd 5107, London: HMSO.

Lowe, N Murch, M Borkowski, M Weaver, A Beckford, V with Thomas, C (1999) *Supporting Adoption: Reframing the Approach*, London: BAAF.

Murch, M Lowe, N Borkowski, M Copner, R and Griew, K (1993) *Pathways to Adoption*, University of Bristol, Socio-Legal Centre for Family Studies, London: HMSO.

Parker, R (1999) *Adoption Now: Messages from Research*, Chichester: John Wiley & Sons.

Performance and Innovation Unit (2000), *Prime Minister's Review of Adoption*, London: The Cabinet Office.

Reich, D and Batty, D (1990) *The Adoption Triangle*, London: BAAF.

Rowe, J and Lambert, L (1973) *Children Who Wait*, London: ABAA.

Social Services Inspectorate, Department of Health (1996a) *For Children's Sake: An SSI Inspection of Local Authority Adoption Services*, London: Department of Health.

Social Services Inspectorate, Department of Health (1996b) *Voluntary Adoption Agencies Inspections to 31 March 1994, Overview Report*, London: Department of Health.

Social Services Inspectorate, Department of Health (1997) *Better Management, Better Care*, the 6th Annual Report of the Chief Inspector, Social Services Inspectorate, 1996/97, London: Department of Health.

Social Services Inspectorate, Department of Health (1999) *Meeting the Challenges of Changes in Adoption – Inspection of Voluntary Adoption Agencies*, CI(99)7.

Triseliotis, J Shireman, J and Hundleby, M (1997) *Adoption: Theory, Policy and Practice*, London: Cassell.

Aims and methods

This survey is the main study arising from the work of the BAAF Adoption Statistics Project and the objective was to gain a comprehensive picture of the numbers, characteristics and histories of looked after children who were adopted in England during 1998/99.

2.1   The Adoption Statistics Project

The BAAF Adoption Statistics Project was set up in 1996 with the aim of developing information about the characteristics of children subject to adoption, their birth families, and also the profile of their adoptive families. Three studies from the project have already been published.

- A pilot survey of adoptions arranged by local authorities and voluntary agencies was initiated in 1996 and conducted during 1997 to scrutinise important areas of concern in relation to adoption work by local authorities (Dance, 1997).

- The survey was complemented by the analysis of data on children adopted from the care system available from the existing Department of Health *Children Looked After* database, which produced some very important findings concerning the patterns of adoption for looked after children (Ivaldi, 1998).

- The data collected since the mid 1990s by the Social Services Inspectorate (SSI) when inspecting voluntary adoption agencies in England have allowed relevant investigation of issues that dominate adoption practice by the voluntary agencies, and their specific contribution (Ivaldi, 2000).

2.2   Aims and key issues of the study

Although the various pieces of research already conducted for the purpose of this project had contributed towards a better knowledge of adoption out of care, there was still a need for further collection of individual data on the children and their families to inform future adoption practice.

A major aim of the present adoption survey was therefore to gather detailed information concerning issues which had not been addressed in the preceding phases of the project, but were nevertheless of great relevance to social services departments.*

The material collected from local authorities allowed the examination of key issues such as the ethnicity of the children, placement of siblings, children with special needs, placement history and delays in adoption procedures. The data also included detailed information on the profile of both the birth families and the adoptive parents. This permitted the investigation of the actual composition of the adoptive families, and provided figures for single-parent adoption, the child's position in the family and the age gaps between children.

---

* The scope of the study was restricted to non-relative adoptions in England and therefore did not cover the whole spectrum of adoption. Figures in the present study are only relevant to adoptions arranged by local authorities for children who have been looked after by them. This excludes adoption arrangements made exclusively by approved voluntary adoption agencies, step-parent or other relative adoptions and intercountry adoptions. Unless specified otherwise, we use the term "in care" for all children looked after by local authorities, that is, children looked after under Section 31 as well as those accommodated under Section 20 or those who start to be looked after under an emergency protection order.

Moreover, the design of the survey made it possible to cross-tabulate full details of the children adopted with all relevant information concerning their birth parents, the adoptive family that had been found for them, as well as some data relating to the agency which had arranged placement for the particular child.

2.3 Sample and methodology

The adoption survey was planned as a two-stage process of collating reliable information concerning adoption of looked after children. This report concentrates almost exclusively upon the main stage of the survey, but it is important to remember some of the conclusions that were drawn from the preliminary investigation.

2.3.1 The preparatory phase of the survey

The purpose of the preliminary stage of the study was to assess the feasibility of conducting the main survey and to establish whether accurate information could be obtained on adoptions arranged by local authorities. Additionally, there were some important questions relating to local authority organisation, management and policies in relation to adoption.

An area of particular interest was that of the variability in agency adoption practice, and whether it would be possible to identify policy and organisation factors contributing to the variance in the actual volume of adoption work undertaken by local authorities throughout the country. The executive summary of key findings for the above aspects is available from BAAF (Ivaldi, 1999).

This first phase was conducted in March 1998, with a brief questionnaire distributed to all local authorities in England prior to the last wave of local government reorganisation taking place on 1 April (N=133). Nearly 75 per cent of the authorities completed and returned their questionnaire to BAAF.

The findings highlighted some of the practical problems which would arise during the main research and helped ensure the data collection process was compatible with adoption practice in local authorities.

2.3.2 The study samples

In this section, the focus is on some of the methodological problems against which the analysis of the children and family data was set. Before we describe the nature and size of the children and family samples in the study, it is important to mention some aspects of the methodology underpinning the collection of data from local authorities.

Collection of data from local authorities

One lesson drawn from the outcome of the preparatory survey was that any further attempt to collate information should avoid respondents in social services departments having to complete a large number of questionnaires. It was equally important to ensure that details of children were collected in a manner that would allow cross-tabulation with all relevant data concerning their birth family and adopters.

In order to facilitate the task of respondents and reduce the demand placed on local authorities, the existing BAAF assessment Forms E and F were used as a means of gathering individual data on adopted children and both the birth and adoptive families to whom they related. Participating social services departments were asked to provide cross-referenced photocopies of the first sections of Forms E and F together with some of the key dates of the adoption process.

Two important remarks need to be made here. Firstly, the information collected from local authorities did not include any of the narrative assessment material which is usually attached to Form E. Secondly, all efforts were made to ensure confidentiality and anonymity, and to avoid any disclosure of sensitive information regarding the identity of children, families, and agencies. All replies were treated with the utmost confidence and responses were used exclusively for research and statistical purposes. All agencies were given the option of deleting personal identifying details from the forms.

Although Forms E and F were not designed originally to serve research purposes, they are widely used by local authorities, and undoubtedly provide a rich source of information concerning substantive issues in relation to adoption from the public care system.*

Alternative data collection forms were provided for those agencies which were not using BAAF assessment forms or had expressed great concerns regarding confidentiality. These data collection forms were designed to collect similar information to that contained in Forms E and F. Of the 116 participating agencies, a total of 15 used the above survey questionnaires to provide the information in an anonymised manner.

Sampling procedures

The preparatory phase of the study also allowed decisions to be made about the period of time to be surveyed, the selection of relevant adoption cases by responding agencies and the staff and time resources which participation in the main survey would entail.†

Study population

The initial aim was to produce a representative sample of children who had been adopted from the care of local authorities during 1998/99. The study population included 145 of the 150 local authorities in operation at the time of sending out questionnaires.‡

All agencies were sent copies of the survey together with personalised covering letters in March 1999. The follow-up procedure was a two stage process: the first reminder letter was sent out to local authorities who had not replied by June 1999, followed in late August 1999 by a second reminder and a further copy of the survey where requested by respondents.

Clustering of agencies

Local authorities were stratified according to the number of adoption cases carried out during the last financial year. This was based on the DoH report

---

* The SSI inspection of adoption services in 1996 reported that almost all the assessments of children eventually referred to the adoption services were channelled via BAAF Form E (DoH, 1996). Consistent with those findings was that the vast majority (94 per cent) of the authorities who took part in the first stage of the survey were using BAAF Form E. This compared with 62 per cent of the agencies with regard to the use of Form F, but in practice we found that most of them were using Form F when establishing their adopters' records.

† There was some variation in the period of time used for adoption records by agencies, with nearly two-thirds (63 per cent) of local authorities referring to financial year and over a third (37 per cent) of respondents providing adoption figures on the basis of the calendar year.

‡ A total of 5 authorities were excluded from the scope of the survey. Three agencies had very few looked after children and, in practice, had not carried out any adoption cases over the past financial year (Rutland, City of London and Isles of Scilly). In two other authorities (Blackpool, Havering), the relevant information was not available at time of sampling (see DoH, *Children looked after by Local Authorities*, Year ending 31 March 1999, England, A/F 99/12, published 2000).

of the numbers of children who left the care of local authorities for the purpose of adoption. All agencies were grouped into four homogeneous categories based on quartiles for the total number of adoptions arranged during the last year of statistics (see Table 2.1 below).*

Adoptions reported by DoH	Number of agencies	Per cent	Number of cases requested	Size of target sample
1 to 6 adoption(s)	40	28	4	160
7 to 11 adoptions	38	26	9	342
12 to 20 adoptions	39	27	15	585
More than 20 adoptions	28	19	20	560
TOTAL	145	100	N/A	1,647

Table 2.1

Sample selection: categories by number of adoptions (Quartiles)

Source: DoH, *Children looked after by Local Authorities*, Year ending 31 March 1997, England, A/F 98/12, 1998.

Selection of cases and period of time for returns

In the light of conclusions drawn from the preparatory stage of the research, local authorities were asked to supply a sample of their most recent adoption cases, the size of which was equal to the cluster centre or group mean expressed in number of adoptions (see Table 2.1 above).

The rationale for this decision about sampling was twofold: first, it was evident from the comments made by respondents to the initial phase of the survey that the likelihood of their taking part in the main stage was largely dependent upon the amount of work and time that would be required to supply the information. The second reason was that not only was it easier to retrieve records for the most recent cases dealt with by the agency, but also the selection of the latest adoption cases helped overcome the problem of having to define a period of time common to all agencies.

The guidance notes for completion of the survey provided a clear definition of cases of "agency adoption" falling into the scope of the survey by referring to 'adoption orders already made, where the child concerned was looked after by your agency, whether the child was placed by your agency, another authority or a voluntary agency (exclude intercountry adoptions and inter-agency placements arranged by your agency when the child was looked after by another authority)'.

Of particular relevance to the sampling approach was the analysis of adoption practice by local authorities. Previous exploration of data on looked after children had highlighted patterns of adoption work undertaken by the agencies, one of the significant findings was the consistency of numbers of adoptions over time by local authorities.†

From those findings it could be assumed that the latest adoption cases would not only be comparable to a randomly selected sample, but would also

---

* DoH data were available for 113 authorities. Missing figures for 7 local authorities were extracted from the preparatory phase of the survey. Additional figures were collected over the phone from 13 new unitary authorities, and estimated from total numbers of looked after children at 31 March 1998 in another 13 agencies who came into existence on 1 April 1998 (simple linear regression model with adjusted R^2=0.77 at p<0.001).

† Analysis of numbers of children adopted from local authorities over the 1994–98 period of time revealed a high level of consistency in the volume of adoption work undertaken by individual authorities. Linear bivariate correlation coefficients showed little variation and were as follows: years 1994/95 and 1995/96 r=0.83; 1995/96 and 1996/97 r=0.84; 1996/97 and 1997/98 r=0.88. All correlation coefficients significant at p<0.01 (2-tailed) (DoH 1993–97 *Children looked after by local authorities* data).

provide a fairly good representation of the agency "average" caseload in a typical year.

In the 28 large authorities with more than 20 adoptions a year, limitations were imposed on the process of collecting data by the inevitable constraints of agency staffing and resources. This led to a decision to limit the cases asked for to 20, thereby reducing the demand placed on respondents. It was assumed that these 20 cases would be statistically representative of all adoption cases the agency had dealt with over the last year of reference.*

Implications of sampling and the use of grossing up factors

One major implication of the sampling procedure employed in the main survey was the need for designing appropriate weighting factors within each agency. This was particularly important in those large authorities which had provided a limited number of adoption cases, and whose relative weight in the sample would have been significantly under-represented without the use of multiplying factors.

All figures presented in this study were derived from the local authority case returns grossed up using aggregate data for the whole cohort of children leaving care for adoption during 1998/99. The latter statistics were extracted from the *Personal Social Services Performance Assessment Framework* (PSS/PAF) (DoH, 2000) database which represents a very reliable source of information about the performance of each local authority social services department with regard to adoption of looked after children.

Two essential methodological observations must be made. First, all values of the weighting variable were estimated at the local authority level according to the number of adoptions reported to the DoH for the purpose of performance assessment. Second, the above weighting of cases applied exclusively to participating agencies: there was no attempt to extrapolate "England" figures by deriving comparable estimates for the authorities which did not respond to the survey.

Participating authorities and the response rate

The final sample consisted of 116 participating authorities. The overall response rate was 80 per cent, which was very satisfactory compared with usual standards of participation in self-administered postal surveys. It must be emphasised that the above rate of participation in the main survey was clearly illustrative of local authorities' increasing commitment to adoption issues and the development of the service for children and families.

The 116 participating local authorities fell into five main types. The first group was composed of 27 shire counties, some of which were large agencies which had been affected by local government reorganisation during the preceding year. The second category consisted of 31 metropolitan districts, while a third category consisted of the 34 unitary authorities of the sample.†

---

* In order to test the hypothesis that the 20 latest adoption cases would not differ significantly from preceding ones, an exploratory analysis of subgroup similarity measures was carried out on the 1996 *Children looked after by local authorities* data employed in previous publication. Cases were gathered in 5 large agencies and clustered into 2 random groups which were compared on 3 key-variables within each authority (age at entry into care, age at placement and age at adoption) by means of two-sample t-tests. Cases were randomly assigned to two groups, so that any observed differences in response were due to how adoptions cases in each groups were actually dealt with by relevant agencies. The observed p values in t-tests revealed that none of the differences of means between sample and control groups were statistically significant across the 5 authorities (all values of $p>0.01$ n.s.).

† In the present study, findings always relate to the newly established agencies, including all unitaries which came into existence between 1995 and 1997 following the successive waves of local government reorganisation. It must be remembered that some of the adoption cases provided by those agencies had been actually dealt with by previous Shire counties prior to LGR (for more information see Herts B (1997), 'Local government reorganisation and children's services in England', *Adoption and Fostering*, 21:2, pp.50–53).

A total of 9 inner London Boroughs took part in the survey, forming the fourth group of agencies. Finally, the fifth group comprised 15 outer London boroughs.

The response rate was very similar across all types of local authority. Although some of the agencies in the sample had undergone considerable change because of local government reorganisation, there was, for example, no clear evidence of a reluctance for the new unitaries to take part in the survey.*

In contrast, there were some significant differences between local authorities according to whether they had taken part in the preparatory phase of the study: of the agencies which had done so, 88 per cent also responded to the main stage survey. This compared with only 65 per cent in the authorities which had not completed the first stage questionnaire.[†] It was interesting that nearly two-thirds of the latter decided nevertheless to respond to the main survey.

The research samples: children, birth families and adopters

The survey sample collected from the responding authorities was made up of 1,330 individual cases of children relating to a total of 1,062 birth / adoptive families.[‡]

When applying the multiplying factors derived from the analysis of the PSS/ PAF data, the children sample totalled 1,801, which represented about 82 per cent of all agency adoptions during 1998/99. The comparable grossed up figure for the family sample was 1,448.

The extent of missing data

From the adoption data published by the DoH, it was possible to estimate the actual extent of missing data in the sample. During the above financial year of statistics, the authorities which had not responded to the main survey had arranged a total of nearly 380 adoptions for their looked after children, that is, 18 per cent of all adoptions from care.**

As we shall see, there were indications that the 1,801 children in the study can be considered as a representative sample of all children adopted from local authority care during 1998/99. With respect to all relevant children's characteristics, comparisons were made with statistics compiled for adoption out of care and published at a national level by the DoH. No significant differences were found in any of the key variables examined in the following chapters.[††]

A considerable amount of information was contained in the local authority returns and the material inevitably included some errors or discrepancies. Obvious discrepancies were corrected prior to the use of records. However, in some cases, part of the information concerning either the children or families was missing. Therefore, on occasion, the analysis had to be restricted to cases where full details were available. All relevant groupings will be detailed in the following chapters of this report.[‡‡]

* χ^2=1.253 df 4 p=0.869 n.s.

† χ^2=8.524 df 1 p<0.01; Cramer's V=0.259.

‡ Each child in a group of siblings counted as a separate case. If the last requested case was part of a sibling group being placed with the same adopter(s), the agency was asked to include all children in the sibling group.

** With regard to the volume of adoption work undertaken during the year of statistics, no significant differences were found between the agencies which responded to the main survey and those which did not (analysis of variance: F=0.951 df 1 p=0.331 n.s.).

†† The same was true when processing checks on the basis of the unweighted sample of 1,330 children. The profile of those children corresponded to figures reported by the DoH for the whole cohort adopted from the public care system during 1998/99.

‡‡ Information was missing for 7 birth families and 28 adopters.

Local authority figures and regional breakdown

Table 2.2 below provides a summary of the number of adopted children by each type of authority in the study, together with the regional make up of the sample. Comparable information is described for both the birth and adoptive families. It should be remembered that children and birth families were exclusively coming from local authorities whilst a number of adoptive families were recruited by voluntary adoption agencies (see the 'other' category Table 2.2).

Children adopted from shire counties and metropolitan disctricts were found in equal proportions (33 per cent) in the sample, whilst adoptions from London boroughs accounted for a total of 12 per cent. Approximately a fifth (22 per cent) of the children adopted during 1998/99 had been placed by unitary authorities. These figures were very similar to those derived for the birth family sample.

Type of authority	Number of authorities	Children N	%	Birth families N	%	Adopters N	%
Shire County	27	598	33	456	31	484	33
Metropolitan District	31	594	33	503	35	432	30
Unitary Authority	34	397	22	313	22	192	13
Inner London Borough	9	102	6	82	6	54	4
Outer London Borough	15	110	6	93	6	62	4
Other*	–	–	–	–	–	226	16
TOTAL	116	1,801	100	1,448	100	1,448	100

Region**	Number of authorities	Children N	%	Birth families N	%	Adopters N	%
North East	11	159	9	128	9	113	8
North West	13	181	10	152	11	120	8
Merseyside	5	45	2	39	3	34	2
Yorkshire & Humberside	12	323	18	268	19	239	16
East Midlands	7	173	10	123	8	127	9
West Midlands	10	166	9	132	9	110	8
South West	12	149	8	121	8	90	6
London	24	212	12	175	12	115	8
Eastern	7	168	9	134	9	125	9
South East	15	225	12	175	12	150	10
Other*	–	–	–	–	–	226	16
TOTAL	116	1,801	100	1,448	100	1,448	100

Table 2.2

Local authority figures and the regional make up of the sample

Notes: * "other" refers here to voluntary adoption agencies and local authorities in Scotland and Wales
** DoH regional breakdown

Differences were found in the adoptive family sample, mostly because of the role played by external agencies such as voluntary adoption agencies in recruiting prospective adopters for looked after children needing adoptive placements. Together with a tiny number of adoptive families approved by social services/social work departments in Wales and Scotland, those cases amounted to a total of 226 adopters, that is, 16 per cent of the sample. Cases of inter-agency placements will be examined in Chapter 4.

References

Dance, C (1997) *Focus on Adoption – A snapshot of adoption patterns in England – 1995*, London: BAAF.

Department of Health (2000) *Personal Social Services Performance Assessment Framework (PSS/PAF)*, 1998/99 London: Department of Health.

Ivaldi, G (1998) *Children Adopted from Care: An examination of agency adoptions in England – 1996*, London: BAAF.

Ivaldi, G (1999) *BAAF Adoption Survey: 1998/99 – Report on the preparatory phase*, London: BAAF.

Ivaldi, G (2000) *Children and Families in the Voluntary Sector: An overview of child placement and adoption work by the voluntary adoption agencies in England 1994–98*, London: BAAF.

Social Services Inspectorate, Department of Health (1996) *For Children's Sake: An SSI inspection of local authority adoption services*, London: Department of Health.

The children's profile and history of care

One important aim of the adoption survey was to explore differences and similarities in terms of children's characteristics and prior experiences of care within the cohort adopted from local authorities during 1998/99.

In the first section of this chapter we look at the profile of the children in the study sample. This includes gender, ethnicity, religious denomination and the number of the child's siblings. In addition, we examine some critical features of the children's special needs with regard to developmental and health problems. The second section concentrates on the children's career in care with regard to the number of moves, continuity of care and types of placement experienced by the children prior to joining their adoptive homes.

The adoption procedures will be considered in Chapter 4 together with important issues relating to each of the key stages of the adoption process. The focus of Chapter 5 will be on the time-scales of placing looked after children for adoption and possible factors which may cause delays in achieving permanency.

3.1 Characteristics of the sample children

This first section explores the characteristics of the 1,801 children adopted from care during 1998/99 by looking at their gender, ethnicity, religion or siblings, as well as any special needs. All issues concerning the age profile of the children will be addressed in the second section in the context of the above characteristics.

3.1.1 Gender of child

Boys accounted for 51 per cent of the study sample. This proportion was very similar to that observed in the children leaving local authority care for adoption over recent years, although the most recent figures published by the DoH showed a small increase in the percentage of girls (52 per cent) in the cohort of children adopted during 1998/99.*

KEY FINDING

Boys accounted for 51 per cent of the adopted children.

The balance of gender was also very similar across all types of local authorities.†

3.1.2 Ethnicity

The vast majority (90 per cent) of the children adopted during 1998/99 were white.**

KEY FINDING

90 per cent of the children adopted during 1998/99 were white. Of the minority ethnic children, nearly three quarters were of mixed parentage.

Of the remaining 172 children of a minority ethnic background, nearly three quarters (73 per cent) were of mixed parentage, another fifth (19 per cent) were African and African-Caribbean, and 8 per cent were Asian children.†† The ethnicity of boys was similar to that of girls.***

---

* See DoH, *Children looked after by local authorities –Year Ending 31 March 1999 – England*, A/F 99/12, published 2000, summary Table H, 1994–99. During the year 1998/99, 55 per cent of all looked after children were boys.

† Authorities were classified into five main groups (see Chapter 2). Chi-Square test: χ^2=5.949 df 4 p=0.203 n.s.

** Nearly all children (99 per cent) were of British nationality with a tiny number of children reported as nationals of other countries, mostly within the Commonwealth, EU member states and the United States.

†† There were no cases of Chinese children in the sample.

*** χ^2=3.167 df 2 p=0.205 n.s.

Notably, children from a minority ethnic background were over-represented in the London area where they accounted for 40 and 22 per cent respectively of all children adopted during 1998/99 in the inner and outer London boroughs (see Figure 3.1). This compared with only 7 per cent in the new unitary authorities, 8 per cent in the metropolitan districts and 5 per cent of the children adopted from shire county agencies.*

Figure 3.1

Adoption of children from a minority ethnic background as a percentage of all adoptions in each type of local authority

Note: * "Minority ethnic" refers here to African, African-Caribbean and Asian, as well as children of mixed parentage. Local authorities were clustered into five main categories. N=1,801 children adopted during 1998/99

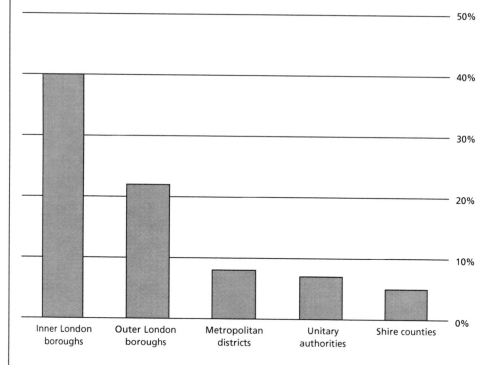

This variation reflected of course the social composition of the population covered by social services departments, particularly in London. Looking at the Local Authority Key Indicators published by the DoH showed that children of minority ethnic groups accounted for 34 per cent of all children aged under 18 years in the inner london boroughs. The comparable figure for the outer London areas was 26 per cent. In contrast, minority ethnic children accounted for only 9 and 4 per cent of the under-18 population in the metropolitan districts and shire counties respectively.[†]

3.1.3 Religion of child

In over a third (36 per cent) of the cases there was no indication of the child's religion. It is likely that these were children for whom religion was of no particular significance to the birth parent(s) and was therefore omitted when completing the forms.

However, these findings raised questions about whether local authorities had asked about religious issues when completing the forms. It must be noted here that Form E allows identification of children with "no religion" by asking case workers to state "What religion, if any, has been specified for the child?".

It should also be remembered that the Children Act 1989 refers to four elements of background and specifically requires that local authorities *'give due consideration to the child's religious persuasion, racial origin and*

> **KEY FINDING**
>
> Children from a minority ethnic background were over-represented in the London area where they accounted for 40 and 22 per cent respectively of all children in the inner and outer boroughs.

> **KEY FINDING**
>
> In over a third of the cases there was no indication on Form E of the child's religion.

* For the purpose of the analysis and to avoid small counts in the cells, the children were grouped in two main categories of ethnicity, i.e. 'white children' (N=1,629) and 'minority ethnic children' (N=172). The latter group included all African, African-Caribbean and Asian children, as well as children of mixed parentage. Differences were statistically significant: χ^2=147.612 df 4 at p<0.01; Cramer's V=0.286.

† See *Local Authority Key Indicators* (1997). Figures were based on the 1991 Census data. It should be noted, however, that there was a wide variation in the proportion of black children across metropolitan districts: for instance, some large urban areas such as Birmingham or Bradford had a percentage of minority ethnic children as high as 30 per cent (35 and 28 per cent respectively).

cultural and linguistic background" (section 22(5)(c)). Similarly, the Adoption Act 1976 states that 'an adoption agency shall, in placing a child for adoption, have regard (so far as in practicable) to any wishes of a child's parents and guardians as to the religious upbringing of the child' (section 7).

	N	% of all cases	% of cases where religious denomination was recorded
None	432	24	38
Church of England	443	25	39
Catholic	160	9	14
Other Protestant*	82	5	7
Muslim	16	1	1
Other	13	0	1
TOTAL	1,146	64	100
Not specified on form	655	36	
	1,801	100	

Table 3.1

Religious denomination of child

Note: As recorded on forms at the time of approval for adoption.

*Other Protestant not Church of England.

Of the 1,146 cases where religious denomination or lack of it was recorded, four in ten (39 per cent) were Church of England; 14 per cent were Catholic; while another 38 per cent had no specific religion; 7 per cent were recorded as being from another Protestant family background and 1 per cent were Muslim (see Table 3.1).

Patterns of religious affiliation did not vary significantly according to the child's gender.*

In contrast, there was some variation when taking account of the ethnic origin of the adopted children. Black children were significantly over-represented in the "other Protestant" group and accounted for a total of 15 per cent of the children in that particular category. Children of mixed parentage were also more frequent amongst the "other Protestant" and, to a lesser extent, the Catholic children: they represented 17 and 7 per cent of all the children in each of those two religious denominations respectively.[†]

KEY FINDING

39 per cent of the children were Church of England; 14 per cent were Catholic; 38 per cent had no specific religion and 7 per cent were from another Protestant family background.

3.1.4 The number of child's siblings

The majority of the children adopted during 1998/99 had at least one birth sibling, either full or half, and the average birth family was composed of three siblings (see Figure 3.2). In terms of the actual structure of the birth family, more than half (56 per cent) of the adopted children had two or more siblings and nearly a quarter (24 per cent) had a single sibling. Only a fifth (20 per cent) of the children in the study had no birth siblings.

There were no clear differences in size of birth families when taking into account the gender or ethnic origin of the child. Differences were not statistically significant when looking at the average size of birth families across the various types of authorities.**

KEY FINDING

More than half of the adopted children had 2 or more siblings and nearly a quarter had a single sibling.

KEY FINDING

Only a fifth of the children in the study had no birth siblings.

* χ^2=8.621 df 3 p=0.035 n.s. N=1,117 children for whom information about religion was available (cases of Muslim and other religions were excluded from calculation because of the very small number of cases falling in those two categories).

† χ^2=87.847 df 6 at p<0.01; Cramer's V=0.198. N=1,117 children for whom information about religion was available. 'Black' refers to African-Caribbean, African and Asian.

** Analysis of variance: gender F=5.022 df 1 at p=0.065 n.s.; ethnicity (3 categories) F=2.293 df 2 at p=0.101 n.s.; type of agency (5 categories): F=1.792 df 4 at p=0.128 n.s.

Figure 3.2

Number of child's siblings

Note: Percentage of all adopted children by number of other children in birth families (N=1,801 children)

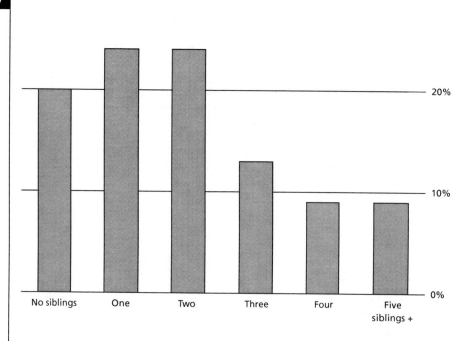

Issues arising from the age profile of the children will be addressed in the second section of this chapter.

3.1.5 Special needs

One important question was whether the children had special needs. There are clear indications from child care research that variables such as physical disability, emotional problems and the child's health condition may account for some significant differences in the success in planning permanency for children in need of a substitute family, and may apply disproportionately to children subject to adoption orders.*

Abuse and neglect: some limitations on the data

Although the empirical information collected from local authorities provided an opportunity to tackle issues related to patterns of special needs, there were some limitations to the extent to which those needs could be assessed and examined. Some areas of uncertainty remained, particularly with regard to problems arising from abuse or neglect as well as the child's emotional or psychological difficulties.

Children who had been identified as sexually abused accounted for 4 per cent of the whole sample, with equal proportions of cases of definite and possible abuse. These cases were more frequent in the older children of the sample (13 per cent of the children aged 5 years and above, as opposed to 2 per cent of the infants aged 6 to 12 months).†

Indications of physical abuse were reported in a total of 6 per cent of the children. There was a linear increase of the proportion of children described as physically abused across age bands, from 1 per cent in the infants aged

KEY FINDING

4 per cent of the adopted children were identified as having been sexually abused. These cases were more frequent in the older children of the sample.

KEY FINDING

Indications of physical abuse were reported in a total of 6 per cent of the children.

* BAAF's recent study of adoption practice by voluntary adoption agencies showed, for example, that nearly two-thirds of the children accepted for placement by the adoption societies were children with special emotional difficulties. A total of 46 per cent were described as having behavioural problems; 41 per cent of the children had developmental needs and 14 per cent were described as having physical impairments (See Ivaldi, G (2000) *Children and Families in the voluntary sector – An overview of child placement and adoption work by voluntary adoption agencies in England 1994–1998*, London: BAAF.).

† Differences were statistically significant: χ^2=97.135 df 8 at p<0.01. Caution should however be exercised because of the small number of children identified as sexually abused. Nearly two-thirds (62 per cent) of the children who had or were likely to have suffered sexual abuse were aged 5 years and over at time of assessment. All of them were looked after under compulsory orders.

under 6 months at time of assessment to 10 per cent in the older children over the age of 5 years.*

Records of poor parenting and neglect were found in 10 per cent of the children adopted during 1998/99 with nearly three quarters (73 per cent) of these cases falling in the 1–4 years age band, and another fifth (19 per cent) aged 5 years and over at time of approval for adoption. Significantly, 92 per cent of these children were looked after by local authorities under care orders. Of the children aged 1 to 5 years, a total of 13 per cent had been subject to poor parenting and neglect.

The above figures were likely to be under-reported on the forms gathered from responding authorities. As we shall see in the second section of this chapter, nearly four in ten of the children adopted during 1998/99 had been initially taken into care because of abuse or neglect. Also, the vast majority of the children adopted during 1998/99 were looked after under a care order when a decision was made that adoption was in the child's "best interest", which may be regarded as one crude but significant indicator of the severity of the child's circumstances.†

One practical reason for under-reporting of abuse and neglect in the survey is that all considerations regarding placement are detailed at length in the narrative material attached to the forms and therefore would not be systematically duplicated in the first section of the document which was used as a means of collecting the data (see methodological considerations in Chapter 2).

More importantly, however, research evidence has suggested that practice falls far short of providing full information about the children's histories and experiences of abuse, particularly when dealing with cases where children had been sexually abused. Farmer and Pollock (1998) found in their study that information about sexual abuse or abusing behaviour had not been passed on to caregivers in approaching half the placements (45 per cent). Similarly, Monck and New (1996), in their study of sexually abused children in treatment facilities, found that social workers did not know about the previous sexual abuse experiences of 40 per cent of the children for whom they held responsibility.

Reasons for information about abuse histories not being passed on to caregivers may include mistaken views about confidentiality, minimisation of the significance of these abuse incidents, and a desire to avoid "labeling" children while, occasionally, information is withheld in order to secure a placement where it is thought that with full knowledge carers might refuse to take a child (Monck and New, 1996).

In the following sections, the emphasis is placed on the categories of needs for which the information was found to be accurate and reliable. This includes developmental problems and/or learning difficulties, the child's health condition, and record of hereditary risks.

Some of the findings bring us also to the definition of "needs". Here it should be borne in mind that all categories were drawn from the actual types of problems recorded on the forms by the different case workers completing them, and were not defined prior to sending the survey to local authorities.

---

* χ^2=28.125 df 4 at p<0.01. Three quarters (75 per cent) of the children for whom there was an indication of physical abuse were over the age of 12 months at time of approval for adoption, and 94 per cent were in compulsory care.

† Common to sections 31, 38, 44 and 46 of the Children Act 1989 relating to care and emergency protection proceedings is the criterion according to which the Court has to be satisfied that the child is suffering or is likely to suffer significant harm.

All efforts were made to include the multiplicity of the child's needs, but findings should nevertheless be treated with some caution.

Developmental problems and learning difficulties

The first category of need related to the child's developmental problems and/ or learning difficulties. It included difficulties such as the need for developmental assessment, for monitoring the child's learning development, the indication of developmental delay, speech or learning difficulties, and special schooling. Of all the children adopted during 1998/99, a total of 17 per cent were described as children having such difficulties.

The extent of developmental needs varied significantly according to the age of the child: developmental difficulties were more frequent in the older children (24 per cent in those aged 30 months and over) when compared with the infants of the sample (10 per cent in the children under 12 months).*

In their study of adoption of older children aged 5 years and over, Lowe and Murch (1999, p.74) found that 30 per cent of all the families in the survey sample had reported "learning special needs" when completing the questionnaire.

Developmental and learning difficulties were more likely to be identified in the white children: 18 per cent of the latter were described as having such problems, as opposed to 7 and 6 per cent of the mixed parentage and black children respectively.[†]

Very few children, however, were subject to statementing under the Education Act 1981. Of the children aged 30 months and over at the time of approval (i.e. cases to which the analysis of the statementing process is the most relevant), only 6 per cent were statemented, with nearly two-thirds (62 per cent) of these children over the age of five years. It should be noted that statementing is frequently started after placement for adoption.

The health condition of child

Although not the main focus of the research, another important area which was scrutinised was the child's medical condition. Again, the information made available through the forms covered a variety of health issues which were subsequently regrouped into three broad categories for the purpose of the analysis. The categories were as follows: moderate health problems, serious health difficulties (including some life-limiting conditions), and congenital risks.[‡]

Figure 2.3 contains information about the children's health problems as derived from the above categorisation.

A total of 15 per cent of the children in the study were described by social workers as having health problems. Of these, two-thirds (66 per cent) were children exhibiting moderate health problems, while another third were

---

* Comparisons were made on the basis of the child's age at best interest decision (5 categories). Differences were statistically significant: χ^2=50.350 df 4 at p<0.01.

† χ^2=12.714 df 2 at p<0.01. Caution must be exercised given the small numbers of mixed-parentage and black children listed with developmental problems (N=9 and 3 respectively). "Black" refers here to African, African-Caribbean and Asian.

‡ The rationale behind those groupings was essentially based on how adopters would respond to different kinds of information about a child, one important assumption being that many adopters would be able to consider children with "moderate health problems", far fewer with "serious health problems". Health problems which cover a continuum of severity, for example cleft palate, were categorised by the mid point.

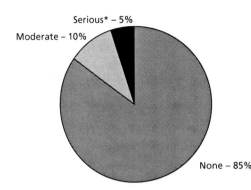

Serious* – 5%

Moderate – 10%

None – 85%

Figure 3.3

The child's health problems

Note: N=1,801 children in the sample; * Serious including life-limiting conditions

described as children with serious medical conditions including some that were potentially life-threatening.*

There was no way of assessing the accuracy and reliability of the above statistics. Looking, however, at comparable figures derived from the Lowe and Murch (1999, p.73) survey of adoption of older children aged 5 years and over showed that "health special needs" were indicated by only 6 per cent of the adoptive families who had completed the survey questionnaire. "Physical special needs" were mentioned by 4 per cent of the adoptive parents participating in the survey.

Turning back to the present study, records of a medical condition were more frequent amongst boys: 18 per cent were listed as children with either moderate or severe medical problems, as opposed to 13 per cent of the girls. Differences were statistically significant, albeit of a low magnitude.[†]

Developmental difficulties were more likely to be found amongst children with severe medical problems: 46 per cent were listed as children presenting developmental difficulties and/or learning difficulties compared with only 19 and 15 per cent of the children with moderate health problems and those with no particular medical record respectively.[‡]

Nearly a fifth (18 per cent) of the adopted children were described as children presenting hereditary risks.**

There were some differences in terms of the child's ethnic origin: congenital risks were more frequent in the children of mixed parentage and, to a lesser extent, the white children in the sample: 26 and 17 per cent respectively of those children had special needs arising from heredity as opposed to only 9 per cent of the black children.[††]

Only a tiny proportion (3 per cent) of the children had both a medical condition and hereditary risks.

Overall, 40 per cent of the children had a developmental or learning difficulty, medical problem or hereditary risk.

KEY FINDING

Records of a medical condition were more frequent amongst boys and less frequent amongst minority ethnic children.

KEY FINDING

40 per cent of the adopted children had at least one special need.

* Moderate health problems included a wide range of concerns such as asthma, mild epilepsy, reflux, sight and hearing difficulties or sacral dimple. In contrast, severe diseases and life-limiting conditions were clustered in the same group, including, for instance, severe brain damage, hepatitis C, blindness, cardiac abnormality, foetal alcohol syndrome or hemiplegia. In a small number of the cases, however, it was not possible to establish with certainty the degree of severity of the child's medical condition. It was assumed that these were general moderate health problems. All necessary checks were performed to ensure that all available data were taken into account.

† Chi-Square statistics: χ^2=12.490 df 2 at p<0.01.

‡ χ^2=60.200 df 2 at p<0.01; Cramer's V=0.183.

** Hereditary risks refer here to a wide spectrum of congenital problems encountered by social workers when preparing the children for adoption. Examples of those difficulties are as follows: hereditary risk of schizophrenia, mother with drug or alcohol dependency, mental health background, family history of heart disease, child carrier of Factor X11 deficiency or DiGeorge Syndrome.

†† χ^2=7.841 df 2 at p<0.05 (the 5 per cent level of significance is used here because of the small number of black children in the sample). "Black" refers to African, African-Caribbean and Asian.

3.2 The child's history of care

In this second section we turn to the analysis of the children's placement history in the care system. There are important issues relating to the "quality" and continuity of care services that local authorities provide to the children whose family life has been disrupted and who are consequently looked after in state care. Although the main focus of the survey was adoption of looked after children, the data collected from local authorities provided information about the children's experiences of change and discontinuity while in care.

The first three of the following sections describes the age of the children at first entry into the public care system, the reason for being taken into care, and their legal status both at time of entry and completion of the assessment process. We then move on to examine patterns of career in care by looking at the child's number of placement changes and returns home. Issues relating more specifically to the types of placement secured for the adopted children over their care history will be addressed in the final part of this section.*

Table 3.2

Age of the adopted child when he/she started to be looked after (categories)

Note: *DoH figures derived for all looked after children adopted during the year ending 31 March 1995–1999 (unpublished). Data from SSDA 903 (one-third sample in 1998 and 1999) were not grossed up. Where there was more than one separate period of care, age at date of first entry in first period of care has been used.

	BAAF Adoption Survey 1998/99		DoH figures 1998/99*		Previous years of statistics DoH figures*			
	N	%	N	%	% 1995	% 1996	% 1997	% 1998
Under 1 month	684	38	220	35	27	28	28	32
1–6 months	327	18	113	18	14	16	15	17
6–12 months	181	10	54	9	7	8	9	12
12–30 months	294	16	107	17	20	18	19	18
30 months–5 years	241	13	82	13	20	19	17	16
5 years and more	74	4	45	7	13	12	12	6
TOTAL	1,801	100	621	100	100	100	100	100

3.2.1 Age at entry into care

KEY FINDING

The mean age of starting to be looked after was 1 year and 2 months for all the children adopted during 1998/99.

KEY FINDING

Two-thirds of the adopted children had come into care under the age of 12 months; half of this group were under 1 month.

KEY FINDING

Figures for age at first entry into the public care system showed a substantial increase in the overall proportion of infants since 1996.

The mean age of starting to be looked after was 1 year 2 months for all the children adopted during 1998/99, with a wide range from a few days after birth to over 9 years of age. Infants under 12 months were clearly in the majority and represented two-thirds (66 per cent) of the whole sample. Of these infants, over half (57 per cent) were babies under 1 month of age when taken into care. Entries of older children aged over 5 years accounted for less than 5 per cent of the total. The remaining 29 per cent were aged between 1 and 5 years when first referred to social services (see Table 3.2).

When compared with the outcome of BAAF's previous study of children who left care for adoption during 1996 (Ivaldi, 1998), the above figures for age at first entry into the public care system showed a substantial increase in the overall proportion of infants: the latter represented only 52 per cent of the 1996 cohort as opposed to 66 per cent in the children adopted during 1998/99.[†]

It is important to place the above findings in the context of the whole

---

* As discussed earlier, various studies have underlined the importance of early entry factors for the subsequent development of the child's career within the system. Although it is necessary to assess the circumstances of the child's entry in the system to determine 'why' the adopted child entered care, these questions were outside the scope of this survey. Reasons for entry into care have, however, been documented by previous research (Ivaldi, 1998).

† In the analysis of the 1996 cohort, the mean age at entry in all the adopted children was 1 year and 10 months, ranging from just after birth to about 15 years (see Ivaldi, 1998).

population of children looked after by local authorities. As acknowledged by the recent *Prime Minister's Review of Adoption*, the age of looked after children upon entry to the care system is lower than previously; over the 1994–1999 period there has been a 49 per cent increase in the number of children starting to be looked after under the age of 1 year, compared to the overall increase of 13 per cent (PIU Report, 2000, p. 12 & p. 83).

With regard to children leaving care for adoption, the significance of this change was assessed by deriving comparable figures from local authority routine returns. Exploration of the adoption survey material was complemented by the analysis of the DoH SSDA 903 database for the relevant year of statistics. The latter provided the necessary benchmark for the investigation of age at first entry into care and contributed to further assessing the representativeness of the survey sample. As evident from Table 3.2, the age profile corresponded to the figures reported by the DoH for all looked after children who left care for adoption during 1998/99, with a very similar proportion (62 per cent) of infants under the age of one year.

Examination of the children's age profile at entry into care according to gender or the type of agency looking after the children revealed no significant differences.*

In contrast, there were substantial differences when considering the ethnic origin of the children, their religious denomination and the actual structure of their birth family in terms of the number of birth siblings. With regard to the latter, it was clear from the data that single children with no birth siblings were significantly younger on entry into care: on average these single children had been taken into care aged 5 months as opposed to 1 year 3 months for the children with one or two birth siblings and between one year 6 months and one year 10 months for the children with 3 or 4 siblings respectively.[†]

Children of an "other Protestant" religious background were younger at time of entry into care, with a mean age of 10 months. This compared with 12 months for both the Catholic children and those who were described as having no particular religious persuasion. In comparison, the Church of England children in the study were significantly older on admission to the public care system, with an average age of 1 year 5 months.**

In respect of the child's ethnic origin, one last important finding was that African-Caribbean, African and Asian children adopted during 1998/99 were considerably younger (when compared with those in previous years) when starting to be looked after, with an average age of 4 months (see Figure 3.4).

KEY FINDING

Single children with no birth siblings were significantly younger (5 months) on entry into care.

KEY FINDING

African-Caribbean, African and Asian children were considerably younger (4 months) at entry into care, as opposed to 9 months for the children of mixed parentage and 1 year 2 months for white children.

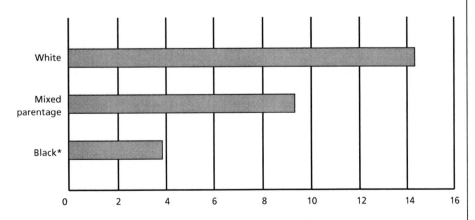

Figure 3.4

Age at entry into care by ethnicity of the children adopted during 1998/99

Note: Months. N=1,801 children in the sample.
* "Black" refers to Asian, African and African Caribbean.

* Analysis of variance for age at starting to be looked after. Gender: F=0.149 df 1 at p=0.700 n.s.; type of local authority (5 categories): F=2.643 df 4 p=0.035 n.s.

† Differences were statistically significant: F=24.633 df 5 at p<0.01

** F=6.640 df 3 at p<0.01. N=1,117 children (categories of "other" religious denomination containing very small numbers of children were excluded from calculation).

This compared with a mean age of 9 months for the children of mixed parentage in the sample, and 1 year and 2 months for white children, the latter category representing, as indicated earlier, the vast majority of the adopted cohort of 1998/99.*

3.2.2 Circumstances at entry into care

Most studies in child care have underlined the importance of early entry factors for the subsequent development of the children's career within the care system (see Packman *et al*, 1996; SSI, 1995).

Whenever possible, it is necessary to assess the circumstances of the child's entry into the system and try to determine "why" the adopted children entered care.

Unfortunately, the design of the adoption survey did not allow investigation of reasons for adopted children being taken into care in the first place. For the purpose of the study, additional figures concerning first reason for looking after the child on entry into care were derived from the DoH Local Authority routine returns for the whole cohort adopted during 1998/99. The latter figures are compared with those derived from BAAF's previous study of children adopted in 1996 (see Table 3.3).

Table 3.3

First reason for being looked after for the adopted children: a comparison between the 1995/96 and 1998/99 cohorts.

Note: *See CLA1996: because of change in legislation on 14 October 1991, this part of the 1996 analysis was restricted to 1,251 children with comprehensive records of care; **Figures derived from DoH Local Authority routine returns. All children adopted from care in 1998/99. Source 903 sample ungrossed (N=621).

Circumstances under which the children were first admitted into care	Children adopted during			
	1995/96*		1998/99**	
	N	%	N	%
Parent's health	74	6	42	7
No parents	7	1	6	1
Child abandoned or lost	30	2	15	2
Family homeless	5	–	–	–
Parent(s) in prison	14	1	3	–
Parents need relief	141	11	81	13
Preventive work with family – concern for child's welfare	116	9	77	12
At request of parent(s) preliminary to adoption	171	14	76	12
Adopted child – breakdown of adoptive placement	–	–	1	–
Child abused/neglected or at risk	488	39	243	39
Child at risk of harm from own behaviour	13	1	3	–
Other reasons	192	15	74	12
TOTAL	1,251	100	621	100

Comparing the two subsets of children over time showed remarkable stability in patterns of reason for starting to be looked after by local authorities. The most common reason for the adopted children being first admitted was "abuse or neglect": overall, cases of possible and definite maltreatment represented a total of four in ten (39 per cent) of the children adopted during 1998/99, which is a similar proportion to that found in the 1996 study.[†]

* F=9.877 df 2 at p<0.01

† It is unfortunate that the data did not allow further clarification of the nature or gravity of the maltreatment. Neither was it possible to determine from the records whether a child was actually suffering ill-treatment or if it was the likelihood of it which justified state intervention.

In 1996, 14 per cent of the adopted children had entered care at the request of parent(s) prior to adoption. This compared with 12 per cent in the 1998/99 group of children leaving care for adoption.

3.2.3 Legal status: from entry into care to assessment

In addition to age at first entry into care and the child's early circumstances, it was also important to consider the legal route by which the adopted children had entered care in the first place. As with the analysis of reasons for first admission, analysis of information about legal proceedings was restricted by the way data had been collected from participating agencies.

The adoption survey did, however, contain comparable information on the child's legal status at time of completion of Form E. For the purpose of assessing how much the legal status had changed, additional figures for first legal status were derived by the DoH for the whole cohort adopted during 1998/99. Details of legal procedures to which children were subject at time of first entry into the public care system are summarised in Figure 3.5, together with comparable figures for the child's legal situation at time of approval for adoption (as derived from the adoption survey).

Of the children adopted during 1998/99, 52 per cent had been first accommodated under a voluntary agreement covered by section 20 of the Children Act. A quarter (25 per cent) of the children first entered the public care system under care orders. Cases of emergency admission amounted to 17 per cent of the total, but it is important to note that such emergency proceedings are short-lived and rapidly become either voluntary agreements or care orders.*

KEY FINDING

12 per cent of the adopted children had entered care at request of parent(s) prior to adoption.

KEY FINDING

52 per cent of the children had been first looked after under a voluntary agreement and a quarter under care orders. Cases of emergency admission amounted to 17 per cent.

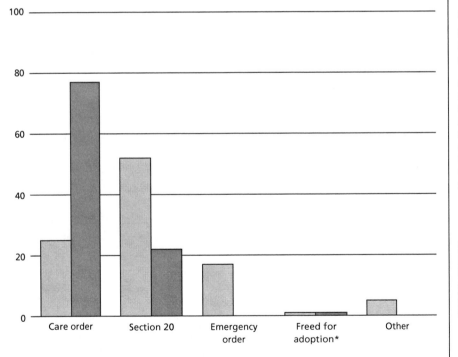

Figure 3.5

Legal status of child: a comparison between first admission into care and approval for adoption*

Note: Percentage of all children adopted during 1998/99. Sources: entry into care: DoH Local Authority routine returns (SSDA 903) third sample, ungrossed figures (N=621); approval for adoption (completion of assessment form E): adoption survey (N=1,801), * Children subsequently freed for adoption are not included.

☐ Entry into care

■ Approval for adoption

These figures were very consistent with those derived for the 1996 cohort of children leaving care through adoption, and confirmed the over-representation of children subject to compulsory care proceedings: when

* Under the Children Act 1989, although there are two major categories of looked after children (voluntary accommodation or care order), there are actually three main routes of entry: children who enter under a voluntary agreement with birth parents (section 20), children looked who are compulsorily admitted under a care order and those who are removed under an emergency protection order (see *A Guide to the Children Act 1989*, 1990, Clarke Hall and Morrison, Law Relating to Children and Young Persons, Special Bulletin, London, Butterworths, Tenth Edition, p.62–107; see also Bainham, A (1990) 'Children, the New Law. The Children Act 1989', Bristol, *Family Law*).

compared with the whole population of children entering care, both care and emergency protection orders were found much more frequently among adopted children.

Not only were care orders much more frequent in the adopted children at time of first entry in the public care system but also the 1996 study found that the circumstances of nearly half of the children initially admitted under voluntary agreement had altered in such a way as to warrant a move to compulsory care. Consequently, cases where children had been the subject of care orders at a later stage in their care history amounted to 75 per cent of the 1996 sample (Ivaldi, 1998).

Analysis of the child's legal status at time of assessment for the 1998/99 cohort showed very similar patterns: consistent with preceding research findings, over three-quarters (77 per cent) of the children adopted during 1998/99 were looked after under a care order at the time of the "best interest" decision of adoption, while only 22 per cent were accommodated under a voluntary agreement (see Figure 3.5). As explained earlier, all emergency protection orders had been either followed by the granting of a care order or replaced by a voluntary agreement with the birth family.

Only a tiny number (1 per cent) of the children were the subject of freeing orders at the time of completing Form E. It should be remembered here that these figures refer solely to the child's status at date of completion of the forms and therefore do not include children who were subsequently freed for adoption at a later stage. The DoH report, *Children looked after by local authorities* (1998/99), showed that freeing orders were clearly an important route to adoption as 33 per cent of the adopted children had been subject to a freeing order at the time of their adoption.*

The association between the child's legal status and special needs arising from abuse or neglect was identified in the preceding section of this chapter. The gender balance was very similar in both the children under compulsory care proceedings and those accommodated under section 20 at time of approval.†

Voluntary agreements were over-represented in the black children of the sample (54 per cent as opposed to 20 per cent of the mixed parentage and 21 per cent of the white children).‡

Interestingly, there were some differences within the group of minority ethnic children. Whilst 31 per cent of the African-Caribbean children were looked after under a section 20 agreement between the social services departments and the birth parents, the comparable figure was 44 per cent for the African children and 93 per cent for Asian children.**

Children subject to voluntary agreements with birth parents were also slightly more frequent in the shire county authorities (25 per cent) and outer London boroughs (26 per cent), while they were less likely to be found in the children adopted from metropolitan districts (16 per cent).††

KEY FINDING

Over three-quarters of the children were looked after under a care order at time of the "best interest" decision of adoption, whilst only 22 per cent were still accommodated under section 20.

KEY FINDING

Voluntary agreements were over-represented in the black children of the sample: 54 per cent as opposed to 20 per cent of the mixed parentage and 21 per cent of the white children.

KEY FINDING

Children subject to voluntary agreements with birth parents were slightly more frequent in the shire county authorities (25 per cent) and outer london boroughs (26 per cent).

---

* There was a significant increase in the proportion of children freed for adoption over time, from 22 per cent in 1994 to 33 per cent in the year ending March 1999. Concurrently, the proportion of children subject to a care order at date of adoption fell from 57 per cent in 1994 to 47 per cent in 1999 (see DoH (2000) *Children looked after by Local Authorities, Year ending 31 March 1999, England*, A/F 99/12,.

† χ^2=0.095 df 1 at p=0.758 n.s.

‡ "Black" refers here to African, African-Caribbean and Asian. Chi-Square test: χ^2=30.212 df 2 at p<0.01.

** These differences were statistically significant: χ^2=34.203 df 3 at p<0.01, Cramer's V=0.447; calculation restricted to the 172 children of minority ethnic background in the sample (excluding white children).

†† χ^2=16.467 df 4 at p<0.01

The age profile of the children compared with legal status was consistent with previous findings: children accommodated voluntarily were aged 8 months on average at time of first entry into care, as opposed to 1 year and 3 months in those looked after under care orders.*

3.2.4 Number of child's placements

How many moves did the adopted children experience throughout their whole time in the public care system? Figures are summarised in Table 3.4 in terms of the actual number of main placements a child had since first entry. Placement for adoption and the initial period at home with birth parents prior to placement are not included in the number of main placements.

	N	%
Single placement	683	38
2	326	18
3	264	15
4	161	9
5	117	6
6 and more	249	14
TOTAL	1,801	100

Table 3.4

Number of child's placements before joining the adoptive family

Note: Figures include all types of placement after the child started to be looked after (e.g. placement with relatives, birth parents, foster carers, hospital, residential accommodation). Both the initial period at home with birth parents and placement for adoption were excluded.

As can be seen from Table 3.4, 38 per cent of the children had a single placement prior to joining their adoptive family. In almost all cases (98 per cent) this was a foster placement. Another fifth (18 per cent) had two placements before they moved with adopters. At the opposite extreme of the scale, more complex patterns of care history were not unusual: children with four placements or more accounted for 29 per cent of the total sample.

No significant variation was observed in placement history with regard to the child's gender or ethnic background.†

On the other hand there were significant differences in terms of legal status and the age of child when taken into care. Children looked after under a care order at time of preparation for adoption had a more complex career in care. Only a third (33 per cent) of those children had a single placement before joining adopters, as opposed to 56 per cent of the children accommodated voluntarily. Only 17 per cent of the latter experienced four or more placements compared with 33 per cent of the children under compulsory proceedings.‡

Only 15 per cent of the children who entered care as babies under the age of 1 month had had four or more placements and more than half (56 per cent) of them had a single placement episode prior to moving to adopters. Interestingly, infants aged 1 to 12 months were over-represented in the group of children with a complex history of care: 44 per cent of them had four or more placements while in care. Older children aged 5 years and over on admission had a different profile with only 16 per cent of these children having four or more placements during their time of being looked after.**

KEY FINDING

38 per cent of the children had a single placement prior to joining adopters. In almost all cases this was a foster placement.

KEY FINDING

Children with four placements or more accounted for 29 per cent of the total sample.

KEY FINDING

44 per cent of children entering care aged 1–12 months had four or more placements before joining adopters.

* Analysis of variance: F=36.612 df 1 at p<0.01

† Analysis of variance. Gender: F=2.836 df 1 at p=0.123 n.s.; ethnicity: F=2.791 df 2 at p=0.062 n.s.

‡ Chi-Square statistics were as follows: χ^2=77.906 df 3 at p<0.01; Cramer's V=0.208

** χ^2=215.189 df 9 at p<0.01; Cramer's V=0.200

3.2.5 Returning home

As significant as the total number of a child's moves within the system is their experience of discharge and re-entry into care. There are important concerns about the disruptive impact of moves between carers and birth families and it was important to assess the extent of multiple entries.

It was evident from the data that the vast majority (79 per cent) of the adopted children had a continuous career in care and had not returned home during their time of being looked after by local authorities. Another 12 per cent had gone back to their birth parents on one occasion, and 9 per cent had two re-entries. This was remarkably consistent with BAAF's previous investigation (Ivaldi, 1998) of the children leaving care for adoption during 1996.*

Proportions of children discharged, and subsequently re-admitted to care, are contained in Figure 3.6 in the context of the child's ethnic origin. The white and mixed parentage children were more likely to have returned home at least once during their history of care (22 per cent and 21 per cent respectively) whilst only 2 per cent of the black children had experienced discharge.[†]

Children looked after under a care order were more likely to have returned home at least once (23 per cent) and those aged between 1 month and 5

> **KEY FINDING**
>
> **79 per cent of the adopted children had never returned home during their time in care.**

> **KEY FINDING**
>
> **The white and mixed-parentage children were more likely to have returned home at least once: 22 and 21 per cent respectively against only 2 per cent of the black children.**

Figure 3.6

Number of returns home (to birth parents) by ethnic origin of child

Note: Percentage of children with one or two discharges from care within each ethnic category. Figures exclude initial placement at home with birth parents, but include all moves from other relatives to birth parents (N=1,801 children).
* "Black" refers to African-Caribbean, African and Asian.

% with one discharge

% with two discharges

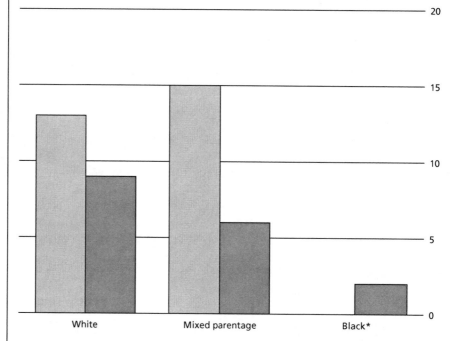

years on entry (31 per cent). In contrast, children accommodated under section 20 were found to have a significantly lower number of discharges (13 per cent), as had the very young babies aged under 1 month at first referral to local authorities (9 per cent). There were no clear differences in terms of the child's gender or originating agency.[‡]

* The latter study found that multiple admissions to care were a relatively unusual experience, with nearly 8 out of 10 children having had an uninterrupted history of care (see *Children Adopted from Care* – An examination of agency adoptions in England – 1996, London, BAAF, 1998).

† χ^2=13.107 df 4 at p<0.01.

‡ Relevant Chi-Square statistics were as follows: Gender: χ^2=4.679 df 2 at p=0.096 n.s.; Type of authority (5 categories): χ^2=17.166 df 8 at p=0.058 n.s.; Legal status: χ^2=17.798 df 2 at p<0.01; Age on admission into care: χ^2=115.746 df 6 at p<0.01; Cramer's V=0.179

3.2.6 Types of placement while in care

This last section explores the type of accommodation provided for the children prior to placement with their adoptive families. The information about placements contained in Table 3.5 reflects the proportion of children who have experienced each type of placement at some stage in their care history. For the purpose of the analysis, placements were grouped into five broad categories: placements with birth parents, placements with relatives, foster placements, residential accommodation and hospital placements. Additionally we looked at the extent of disruption of adoptive placements.

| | Type of placement | | | | | | | | | | |
| | With birth parents* | | With relatives | | Foster placements | | Residential accommodation | | Hospital placements** | | Disrupted adoptive placements | |
	N	%	N	%	N	%	N	%	N	%	N	%
None	122	7	1,521	84	18	1	1,714	95	1,599	89	1,774	98
Single	1,188	66	227	13	968	54	79	4	178	10	27	2
2	259	14	37	2	395	22	8	1	17	1		
3	191	11	16	1	237	13			8	0		
4	32	2			137	8						
5+	9	1			46	2						
TOTAL	1,801	100	1,801	100	1,801	100	1,801	100	1,801	100	1,801	100

Table 3.5

All types of placements before adoptive placement

Note: * "Placements with birth parents" includes initial placements prior to the child starting to be looked after.
** "Hospital placement" refers to stays longer than 3 days and therefore excludes initial stay of mother and child after birth.

Children adopted during 1998/99 had almost all been in foster care: nearly all (99 per cent) of them had at least one placement with foster carers during their time in care. On the other hand, only a tiny proportion (5 per cent) of the children had ever experienced residential accommodation. Turning to placements with other adults in the extended family, 16 per cent of the adopted children had been placed with relatives at some point during the course of their stay in the public care system.

Again these findings confirmed the key figures drawn from the analysis of the 1996 cohort of children leaving care for adoption. Also consistent with previous investigation of the DoH database, only 2 per cent of the children adopted during 1998/99 had experienced a breakdown of previous adoptive placement. Those children had been placed with prospective adopters in the course of their care history and then had been subsequently removed from placement by the relevant authorities.

It is of course essential to recognise that the collected information relates solely to children who were successfully adopted during that particular year of statistics and therefore is likely to mask a higher disruption rate in relation to all children placed for adoption by local authorities. For the year ending 31 March 1999, the DoH reported that 82 per cent of all placements for adoption ceasing during the year ended in adoption, while 12 per cent were followed by another placement and were therefore likely to be cases of disrupted adoptive placements (DoH, 2000).

KEY FINDING

99 per cent of the children adopted during 1998/99 had at least one placement with foster carers during their time in care.

KEY FINDING

Only a tiny proportion (5 per cent) of the children had ever experienced residential accommodation.

KEY FINDING

Only 2 per cent of adopted children had experienced a disrupted adoption placement.

References

Department of Health (2000) *Children Looked After by Local Authorities – Year ending 31 March 1999*, England, A/F 99/12, Personal Social Services, Local Authority Statistics, London: Department of Health

Farmer, E and Pollock, S (1998) *Sexually Abused and Abusing Children in Substitute Care*, Chichester: John Wiley & Sons.

Ivaldi, G (1998) *Children Adopted from Care: An examination of agency adoptions in England – 1996*, London: BAAF.

Lowe, N Murch, M Borkowski, M Weaver, A Beckford, V with Thomas, C (1999) *Supporting Adoption: Reframing the Approach*, London: BAAF.

Monck, E and New, M (1996) *Report of a Study of Sexually Abused Children and Adolescents and of Young Perpetrators of Sexual Abuse who were Treated in Voluntary Agency Community Facilities*, London: HMSO.

Performance and Innovation Unit (2000), *Prime Minister's Review of Adoption*, London: The Cabinet Office.

Packman, J Randall, J and Jacques, N (1986) *Who Needs Care?*, London: Blackwell.

Social Services Inspectorate (1995) *Children in Need, Report of an SSI National Inspection of SSD Family Support Services 1993/95*, London: Department of Health.

The adoption process

Previous child care research has drawn attention to the importance of considering adoption as a continuing process, and not a single discrete event. Important issues dominate adoption practice throughout the process of transferring parental responsibility from birth to adoptive families and there are many stages reached and decisions taken on the future of the child in care, prior to being placed for adoption.

The survey data collected from local authorities permitted the exploration of some of the most salient issues in relation to the adoption of looked after children. In this chapter, the emphasis is more specifically on the placement and adoption procedures which start with the assessment and identification of children in need of an adoptive placement.

We look first at the age profile of the children at the various stages of the process. We then turn to the analysis of patterns of adoption in terms of placement of sibling groups, adoption of children of minority ethnic backgrounds, the extent of foster carer adoption in the sample and inter-agency placements.

4.1 Age of the child at the various stages of the process

We begin with an overview of the children's age profile at each of the key transitional stages in the placement history leading from entry into care to the making of the adoption order. The analysis makes relevant comparisons with the data published at a national level. For the purpose of the analysis, we have distinguished between five stages of the process which can be specified as follows:

- entry into care: when the child first started to be looked after*;
- "best interest": decision by adoption agency, following consideration of the adoption panel's recommendation, that adoption is in the best interest of the child†;
- matching: decision by adoption agency, following consideration of the adoption panel's recommendation, that particular adopter(s) are suitable adoptive parent(s) for a particular child;
- placement: when the child started to live with the prospective adopters, or, in the case of existing foster carers, when the foster placement became a placement for adoption;
- adoption: the making of the adoption order by the court.

These steps to adoption provided a useful framework for approaching areas of interest in relation to the average age of the children at each of the successive stages.

4.1.1 Age at "best interest" decision

Although the child's experience of care begins with the first entry into the public care system, it is true to say that the process of adoption itself begins with the identification and assessment of children needing a new family and the resulting decision regarding the child's "best interest". On average, the

KEY FINDING

On average, children were 2 years 6 months old when the decision regarding adoption was made by the relevant local authority.

---

* As derived from the information contained in the assessment forms (see Chapter 3).

† Local authorities were provided with a guidance note for completion of the adoption survey, but it was not always clear whether the returns received indicated the date of the agency decision or of the adoption panel recommendation, where these were different. However, in practice, although the two are distinct stages of the process, the date of the recommendation is unlikely to be separated from the date of the decision by more than a few days.

Figure 4.1

Age of children at time of "best interest" decision

Note: Months. N=1,783 children (data were missing in 18 children).

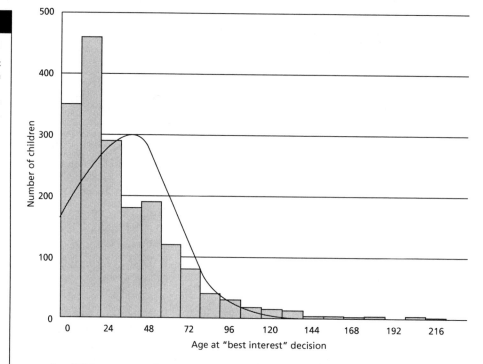

sample children were 2 years 6 months old when the decision regarding adoption was made by the relevant local authority. Age of child at time of "best interest" decision ranged from a few days after birth to about 17 years.

As can be seen from Table 4.1, half (50 per cent) of the children were aged between 1 and 4 years at time of "best interest" decision by the relevant agency. Another third (36 per cent) of the adopted children were infants under the age of one year, whilst older children aged 5 years and over were in the minority (14 per cent of the total).

Table 4.1

Age of child at "best interest" decision (categories)

Note: Data were missing in 18 children of the sample (N=1,783).

Age of child at "best interest" decision	N	%
Under 6 months	351	20
6–12 months	287	16
12–30 months	460	25
30 months–5 years	439	25
5 years and over	247	14
TOTAL	**1,783**	**100**

4.1.2 Age at placement

In any analysis of the outcome of adoption, the age of child when placed is a very influential factor. The mean age at matching was 3 years, with placement taking place on average one month later.

Age at placement ranged from 2 weeks to 17 years and 10 months. Consistent with previous findings concerning age at entry, the children adopted during 1998/99 were substantially younger at placement than those who had been adopted in 1996.*

Details relevant to age groups at matching and placement are summarised for information in Table 4.2. Given that matching took place on average four

---

* BAAF's analysis of the 1996 cohort found that those children were on average 3 and a half years old when placed with adopters (see Ivaldi, 1998).

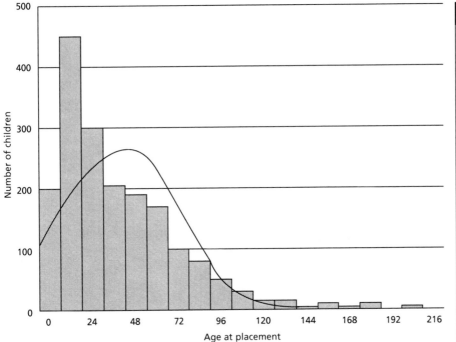

Figure 4.2

Age of children at time of placement with adopters

Note: Months. N=1,783 children (data were missing in 18 children)

weeks before placement, the following part of the analysis concentrates exclusively on the age profile of the children at time of joining the adoptive families.*

Age of child	Matching		Placement	
	N	%	N	%
Under 6 months	222	12	192	11
6–12 months	259	15	259	14
12–30 months	489	27	496	28
30 months–5 years	457	26	460	26
5 years and over	357	20	376	21
TOTAL	1,783	100	1,783	100

Table 4.2

Age of child at matching and placement with adopters (categories)

Note: Data were missing in 18 children of the sample (N=1,783)

As shown in the above data, only 11 per cent of the children were under the age of 6 months when placed with adopters, and only a quarter (25 per cent) had joined their adoptive family before the age of one. Over half (54 per cent) of the children in the sample were aged between 1 and 5 years. Cases of children placed over the age of 5 years accounted for another fifth (21 per cent) of the total.[†]

4.1.3 Age at adoption

The children in the study were, on average, aged 4 years 3 months when the adoption order was granted by the court. This confirmed the downward trend in age at adoption since the mid 1990s: in 1995, the mean age at adoption was 5 years 9 months.[‡]

KEY FINDING

A quarter of the children were under the age of 12 months when placed with adopters. Over half were aged between 1 and 5 years.

KEY FINDING

The mean age of children at adoption was 4 years 3 months.

KEY FINDING

The study confirmed the downward trend in age at adoption since the mid 1990s.

---

* The term "placement" refers here to placement with the adoptive family, either new adopters with whom the child was placed with a view to adoption or fostering families with whom the child was already well settled. In the latter, "date of placement" refers to the date when the foster placement was turned into an adoptive placement by the relevant agency.

† The analysis of the 1996 cohort found that nearly half of the children (46 per cent) were aged 1 to under 5 when placed and that only 15 per cent had been placed with adopters before the age of six months. At the opposite extreme of the age scale, late placements of children aged five and over represented 28 per cent of the whole sample (see Ivaldi, 1998).

‡ In particular, there has been a gradual fall in the proportion of children aged 5 years and over at adoption (see Department of Health (2000), *Children looked after by Local Authorities, Year ending 31 March 1999, England*, A/F 99/12, Table H, p.45).

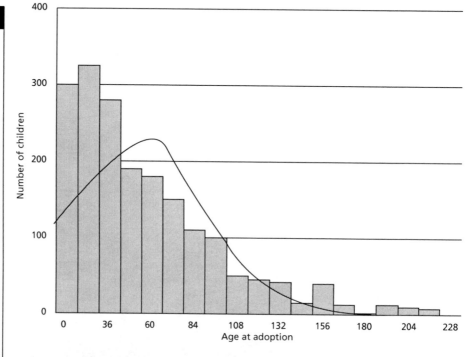

Figure 4.3

Age of children at adoption

Note: Months. N=1,783 children (data were missing in 18 children).

Table 4.3

Age of child at adoption

Note: Data were missing in 18 children of the sample (N=1,783). Categories as used by the DoH in *Children looked after by local authorities*.

Age of child	BAAF Adoption Survey		DoH CLA 1998/99 Figures	
	N	%	N	%
Under 1 year	123	7	200	9
1–4 years	1,051	59	1,250	57
5–9 years	510	29	580	26
10–15 years	92	5	150	7
16 years and over	8	–	10	–
TOTAL	1,783	100	2,200	100

As illustrated in Table 4.3, adoptions arranged by local authorities in England during 1998/99 covered a wide range of cases including adoption of babies under the age of 12 months, as well as adoption of older children.

The peak age at adoption was 1–4 years, with 59 per cent of the children falling into that specific age band. A total of 29 per cent of the children adopted during 1998/99 were aged between 5 and 9 years, while children in their early teens were in the minority (5 per cent). Adoptions of infants under the age of 12 months represented less then 10 per cent of the sample. Again, these findings were very consistent with the national data published by the DoH for the 1998/99 cohort of children leaving care for adoption (see Table 4.3).

4.2 Patterns of adoption

There are some critical issues which will impact on the patterns of adoption for looked after children. Some of the most contentious are placement of sibling groups, transracial adoption, inter-agency arrangements and the involvement of previous foster carers. In addition, this part of the analysis assesses how the birth parents may have responded to the adoption plan for their children.

Although some of these questions relate more specifically to the profile of adoptive families, it was of interest to explore them from the perspective of the children, as there is a need for a clearer picture of the proportions of children affected by the critical issues detailed above.

4.2.1 Placement of sibling groups

Let us begin with the extent of placement of sibling groups. The data collected from local authorities permitted assessment of both the initial placement plan and how the latter was achieved in practice by the relevant local authority (see Table 4.4).

Number of children to be placed for adoption	% Planned*	% Actually placed
Single child placement	62	63
Placement for group of 2 siblings	29	30
Placement for group of 3 siblings	6	5
Placement for group of 4 siblings	2	1
Placement for group of 5 siblings	1	1
TOTAL	100	100

Table 4.4

The extent of placement of sibling groups

Note: N=1,801 children in the sample. No missing data. *As indicated on the assessment form: number of children for whom placement was required

As can be seen, there was no substantial variation between the original plan and the outcome. From the above data it was possible to establish that the actual placement was different to the initial plan in only 4 per cent of the children.

In nearly two-thirds (63 per cent) of the children adopted during 1998/99, placement had been arranged for a single child. This was the plan in a very similar proportion (62 per cent) of the cases. Approximately a third (30 per cent) of the children had been placed as part of a group of two siblings, while placements of groups of three or more siblings accounted for 7 per cent of the sample.

KEY FINDING

34 per cent of the children had been adopted with at least one sibling.

KEY FINDING

The number of children placed for adoption was different to the initial adoption plan in only 4 per cent of the children.

KEY FINDING

In nearly two-thirds of the children placement had been arranged for a single child.

Other siblings in the birth family

The process of data collection did not allow investigation of placements for the remaining birth siblings and concentrated exclusively on the sibling groups adopted during 1998/99. It was possible, however, to identify cases where children had probably been separated from some of their birth brothers and sisters (see Table 4.5).

Of course, the following figures must be treated with extreme caution as they do not include cases of birth siblings who were placed with the same adopters during preceding years. Nor do these figures take account of the age difference between the children, whether they had ever lived together as siblings and whether there were other considerations regarding the needs of other children in the family.

The overall proportion of cases where placement had been achieved for all siblings in the birth family amounted to 37 per cent of the sample. Of the children placed individually, nearly a third (32 per cent) were the only child in the family. Another fifth (19 per cent) had one birth sibling and 22 per cent had three. Over a quarter (26 per cent) of the children placed singly came from birth families comprising four or more children.

For the children placed as part of a pair of siblings, 40 per cent had no other

KEY FINDING

Placement had been achieved for all siblings in the birth family for 37 per cent of the children.

KEY FINDING

Of the children placed individually, nearly a third were the only child in the birth family.

Table 4.5

Placement of sibling groups compared to number of children in the birth family

Note: Percentages within categories of children placed during 1998/99. Children placed as part of groups of 4 and 5 siblings were excluded from the table.

Children placed during 1998/99	Total number of children in the birth family						
	Single	2	3	4	5	6 or more	
Child placed individually	32% (368)	19% (223)	22% (255)	10% (118)	7% (80)	9% (99)	100%
Placement of group of two siblings	–	40% (216)	23% (126)	14% (76)	12% (65)	10% (53)	100%
Placement of group of three siblings	–	–	57% (47)	23% (19)	4% (3)	16% (13)	100%

birth sibling, 23 per cent had one, and over a third (36 per cent) had three or more. For the children placed within groups of three siblings, placement had been secured for all the children in the family in 57 per cent of the cases, while in another 43 per cent there were other birth siblings.*

The importance of maintaining contact with birth siblings had been specifically recorded in only 8 per cent of all the children with birth siblings.

The structure of sibling groups placed during 1998/99

KEY FINDING

Of the pairs of siblings 43 per cent were composed of a boy and a girl, 28 per cent consisted of 2 boys and 29 per cent comprised 2 girls.

Looking at patterns of gender within sibling groups showed some differences (see Table 4.6). Of the pairs of siblings 43 per cent were composed of a boy and a girl, whilst 28 per cent consisted of two boys and another 29 per cent comprised two girls. The sample of larger sibling groups was too small in size to assess the significance of differences in the children's gender.

Composition of sibling groups	% of all sibling groups	% within relevant category
Pairs of siblings		
2 boys	24	28
1 boy + girl	37	43
2 girls	25	29
	86	100
Groups of 3 siblings		
3 boys	2	19
2 boys + 1 girl	3	27
2 girls + 1 boy	4	31
3 girls	3	23
	12	100
Groups of 4 siblings		
2 boys + 2 girls	1	100
Groups of 5 siblings		
3 boys + 2 girls	0.5	50
1 boy + 4 girls	0.5	50
TOTAL	100	100

A total of 11 per cent of the children within sibling pairs were twins. The age gap in the pairs was 1 year 11 months on average, with a maximum of about 9 years 10 months and a standard deviation of 1 year 5 months. In the groups composed of three siblings, the mean age difference between the children was 2 years, ranging from 9 months to 4 years 2 months.

* In the tiny number of cases where children had been placed as part of groups of 4 or 5 siblings, placement had been secured for all the children in the family.

Sibling groups and children placed individually: a comparison

Did children placed as part of sibling groups have a distinctive profile with regard to their characteristics, previous experiences of care and special needs? For the purpose of this analysis, children were grouped into two main categories: children placed alone and those placed within a group of at least two siblings. These were compared on gender, ethnicity, age at first entry into care, legal status, special needs and patterns of career in care. Details are summarised in Table 4.7.

Characteristics	Children placed		Chi-Square Statistics			
	Individually	As part of a sibling group	χ^2	df	Sig.	Cramer's V
Gender						
% of boys	52	49	1.810	1	0.179	n.s.
Ethnicity						
% white	89	93	14.098	2	p<0.01	0.081
% black*	8	6				
% mixed parentage	3	1				
Age at first entry into care						
% under 1 month	51	16	308.028	3	p<0.01	0.414
% 1 to 12 months	29	26				
% 1 to 5 years	18	51				
% 5 years and over	2	7				
Legal status at assessment						
% voluntary agreement	28	10	83.470	1	p<0.01	0.215
% care and freeing orders	72	90				
Special needs						
% developmental / learning	17	16	0674	1	0.412	n.s.
% congenital risks	20	15	7.181	1	p<0.01	0.063
Health problems						
% moderate	9	7	24.295	2	p<0.01	0.116
% serious	11	2				
Abuse						
% physically abused	5	8	5.493	1	0.025	n.s.
% sexually abused**	4	4	2.452	1	0.451	n.s.
Placement history						
% single placement	43	29	38.529	3	p<0.01	0.146
% no return home	83	72	29.639	2	p<0.01	0.128

Table 4.7

The profile of children placed individually and within sibling groups

Note: Children were grouped into 2 main categories: placed individually and placed as part of a sibling group; percentages within each group.
* "Black" refers to African Caribbean, African and Asian.
** Records of "possible" and "definite" sexual abuse were grouped together in order to avoid small counts.

No significant differences were observed in the children's profile with regard to the balance of gender, the presence of developmental problems and/or learning difficulties, and the extent of both physical and sexual abuse (see all relevant Chi-Square statistics in Table 4.7).

There were some differences, albeit of a low magnitude, in terms of the child's ethnicity, congenital risks, health problems and placement history while in care. Children placed with siblings were more likely to be white children (93 per cent as opposed to 89 per cent in the children placed individually). These children also had a more complex history of care: only 29 per cent of them had a single placement before joining adopters (as opposed to 43 per cent of the children placed singly) and 72 per cent had never returned home (compared with 83 per cent in the single children). In contrast they were found to have fewer medical problems, either moderate or severe, when compared with the children placed individually.

Looking at the children's legal status at time of assessment for adoption and age at first admission into care revealed sizeable differences between the two

KEY FINDING

Children placed with siblings were slightly more likely to be white: 93 per cent as opposed to 89 per cent in the children placed individually.

categories of children considered for the analysis. Children placed as part of sibling groups were substantially older at entry into care, with over a half (51 per cent) aged between 1 and 5 years on admission, as opposed to 51 per cent of the single children aged under 1 month.

Compulsory care proceedings were over-represented in the sibling groups (90 per cent as opposed to 72 per cent of the children placed individually).

One last observation was that of the variation found in the extent of placement of sibling groups across the main types of local authority considered for the analysis. Although of a lower magnitude, differences were found to be statistically significant and showed an over-representation of children placed with siblings in the shire counties (43 per cent) and unitary authorities (41 per cent) of the sample. The comparable proportions were of 34, 29 and 28 per cent in the inner London areas, metropolitan districts and outer boroughs of London respectively.*

Importantly, all the above differences continued to be statistically significant when controlled for the subset of 1,435 children who had at least one birth sibling.

4.2.2 Considerations of culture, religion and ethnicity

There are critical issues concerning the linking and placement of children from minority ethnic groups. Although many agencies have a "same race" matching policy which aims to place children with adopters of a similar ethnic background, there is a wide range of approaches that seem to be evident in practice.[†]

In most cases ethnic matching would be the preferred option but various circumstances could lead to a departure from that policy. The multiple complexities of 'ethnic matching' have been exposed in previous child care research (Parker, 1999, p.42–44).

Consideration given to the ethnic and religious matching of child

With regard to all children adopted during 1998/99, local authorities were found to have given special consideration to the child's ethnic background in 37 per cent of the cases. The child's religious persuasion was noted to have been considered in 17 per cent of the children at the time of approval for adoption.

A pattern of association between ethnic and religious needs was found: 31 per cent of the children for whom the relevant agency was considering the necessity for ethnic matching also had a special requirement regarding placement with adopters of same religious background (as opposed to only 8 per cent in the children with no particular need for ethnic matching recorded).[‡]

Looking at patterns of special need arising from the child's ethnic origin, there were significant differences between the white and minority ethnic children of the sample. The priority attached to finding adopters of a similar ethnic background was evident in 63 and 72 per cent of the mixed parentage and black children respectively. The comparable figure for the white children was 34 per cent (see Figure 4.4).**

* χ^2=29.722 df 4 at p<0.01; Cramer's V=0.128.

† One aim of the preparatory stage of the adoption survey was to seek a clearer picture of policy factors that might reveal the degree of commitment to adoption by local authorities. The study showed that 80 per cent of local authorities had set out a policy statement for placement of children in accordance with the Section 22 of the Children Act 1989. Only 52 per cent however had a specific policy statement for placement of black children with a family of similar ethnic origin (see the preparatory stage of the survey).

‡ These differences were statistically significant: χ^2=157.261 df 1 at p<0.01; Phi=0.295.

** χ^2=68.938 df 2 at p<0.01; Cramer's V=0.196

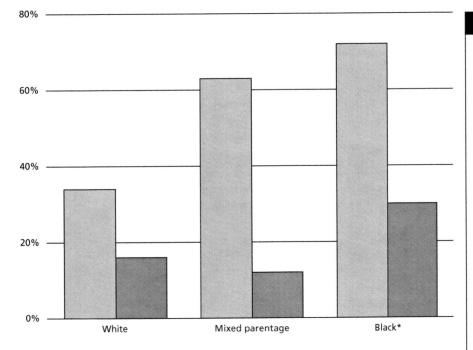

Figure 4.4

Special considerations regarding placement of child with adopters of a similar ethnic and religious background by ethnic origin of the child

Note: As recorded by case workers on assessment material. * "Black" refers to African, African Caribbean and Asian. Percentages of children within each category of ethnicity (N=1,801).

% of children listed with a "same ethnic background" consideration

% of children listed with a "same religious background" consideration

In contrast, analysis of the child's religious needs revealed no similar variation according to ethnicity, although religious considerations were found in a greater proportion (30 per cent) amongst the Asian, African and African-Caribbean children of the sample (see Figure 4.4).*

As can be seen from Figure 4.5, there was also a wide variation in the extent to which local authorities had recorded "same race placement" considerations. Significantly, there was a greater propensity for inner London boroughs (66 per cent of the children) and, to a lesser extent, shire county authorities (48 per cent) to give special consideration to ethnic matching of the child. In contrast only 18, 33 and 38 per cent of the new unitary authorities, metropolitan districts and outer London boroughs respectively had indicated their preference for linking the children with adopters of a similar ethnic background.†

As explained earlier, the high representation of minority ethnic children is a typical feature of the inner London boroughs and may contribute to explaining the higher rate of consideration given to "same race" placement for black and mixed-parentage children.

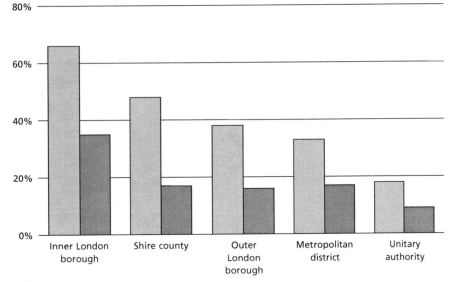

Figure 4.5

Special considerations regarding placement of child with adopters of a similar ethnic and religious background by type of local authority

Note: As recorded by case workers on assessment material. Percentage mentioned "Child should be placed with adopters of a similar ethnic/religious background" within each type of agency (N=1,801).

% of children listed with a "same ethnic background" consideration

% of children listed with a "same religious background" consideration

* χ^2=8.328 df 2 p=0.016 n.s.

† χ^2=134.036 df 4 at p<0.01; Cramer's V=0.273

Turning to the child's need for placement with adopters of a similar religious background, it was interesting to note that significant deviation from sample average was only found in the children adopted from the inner London boroughs and unitary authorities (see Figure 4.5 above). The former had the highest proportion (35 per cent) of religious needs, while special consideration to religious needs had been given in only 9 per cent of the latter group of children.*

Removing children with no particular religion from calculation showed some differences in the extent to which local authorities had considered the need for religious matching across the three main categories of religious denominations in the children adopted during 1998/99.

Religious considerations were over-represented in the Catholic children of the sample (48 per cent), whilst the lowest percentage of such religious needs was found in the other Protestant children (27 per cent). A total of 37 per cent of the Church of England children had special requirements regarding placement with adopters of a similar religious background.[†]

The extent of transracial adoption

Analysis of placement data revealed that transracial adoptions took place for about 2 per cent of all children adopted during 1998/99. It is important to note, however, that the vast majority (90 per cent) of placements arranged by local authorities were for white children with white adopters – either single or a couple. Looking more specifically at patterns of "ethnic matching" for the sub-group of minority ethnic children helped better assess the extent of transracial placement (see Table 4.8).

KEY FINDING

Religious needs were taken into consideration for 48 per cent of Catholic children but were considered less significant for other Protestant children (27 per cent).

KEY FINDING

90 per cent of the placements arranged by local authorities were for white children with white adopters – either single or a couple.

Table 4.8

Patterns of adoption for minority ethnic children

Note: percentage within each ethnic group. *"Black" refers to African-Caribbean, African and Asian in both the children and adopters (N=168, missing data in 4 minority ethnic children)

Ethnicity and status of adopters									
Children	Single white	Couple both white	Single black*	Couple both black*	Single mixed parent-age	Couple one white one mixed parentage	Couple one white & one black*	Couple both mixed parent-age	Couple one black & one mixed parentage
Mixed parentage (120)	1%	27%		10%	4%	22%	35%	1%	1%
Black* (48)	2%		6%	50%	33%	4%	2%		2%

As can be seen from the Table 4.8, only 2 per cent of the African-Caribbean, Asian and African children (one child) had been placed with new parents who were white. Half (50 per cent) had joined black couples, while another third (33 per cent) had been placed with a single adopter of mixed parentage. In contrast there was a substantial proportion (28 per cent) of the children with a dual heritage who had been adopted transracially, mostly by couples where both partners were white.

Not surprisingly records of "same race placement" considerations by the relevant local authority were found to be less frequent in the mixed-parentage children adopted transracially (47 per cent in the former as opposed to 67 per cent of the other children in the same ethnic group).[‡]

KEY FINDING

Only 2 per cent of the African-Caribbean, Asian and African children had been placed with new parents who were white.

KEY FINDING

28 per cent of the children with a dual heritage had been adopted transracially, mostly by couples where both partners were white.

KEY FINDING

Mixed parentage children who were adopted transracially were found to be twice as old (3 years 5 months) as the rest of the mixed-parentage children at time of "best interest" decision.

* χ^2=40.569 df 4 at p<0.01; Cramer's V=0.150.

† χ^2=11.219 df 2 at p<0.01; Cramer's V=0.128. N=684 children of a religious denomination. The sample of children falling into other religious categories was too small to assess the statistical significance of between-group differences.

‡ χ^2=4.957 df 1 at p<0.01

Some caution must be exercised, however, given the size of the sub-sample of children considered for this part of the analysis.

In respect of these mixed parentage children, there was no empirical evidence of significant differences in profile between those adopted transracially and those who had been matched with adopters of a corresponding ethnic background.*

Some of the reasons why local authorities had selected white adopters in these cases are probably to be found in delays that may have taken place during the process of assessing the children's needs for permanent substitute placements. Whilst there were no significant differences in the mean age of the mixed parentage children at time of entry into care, those who were adopted transracially were found to be twice as old as the rest of the children at time of "best interest" decision (3 years 5 months as opposed to 1 year 9 months in the other children of mixed parentage).†

More importantly, perhaps, there was a significant relationship between transracial adoption for mixed-parentage children and the degree of involvement by previous white foster carers. The proportion of carers adopting their foster child amounted to 27 per cent of all cases of children with a dual heritage placed with white adopters, as opposed to only 3 per cent of the other children of dual heritage placed with adopters of a similar ethnicity.‡

KEY FINDING

The proportion of carers adopting their foster child amounted to 27 per cent of all cases of children with a dual heritage placed with white adopters.

4.2.3 Foster carer adoption

From the above findings it is clear that a third question to be addressed from the survey data was that of adoption of looked after children by their foster carers. This represents undoubtedly an important aspect of adoption practice by local authorities, which calls for report and comment.

Cases where foster carers had adopted their foster child accounted for 13 per cent of the children sample.**

KEY FINDING

Cases where foster carers had adopted their foster child accounted for 13 per cent of all the children adopted.

These findings showed a small decrease in the proportion of foster carer adoptions when compared with estimated figures for previous years of statistics.††

In many respects the children adopted by their previous foster carers were not unlike those who had joined a new family for adoption. Differences were restricted to the children's legal status at time of assessment and their age during the successive sequences of the adoption process. With regard to the first of these two aspects, compulsory care proceedings were over-represented in the children adopted by their foster families (85 per cent as opposed to 77 per cent in the rest of the sample children).

KEY FINDING

Compulsory care proceedings were over-represented in the children adopted by their foster families (85 per cent).

But the most striking differences were observed when comparing the age profiles of these two groups of children with children adopted by their previous foster carers being substantially older at each of the key stages of the adoption process (see Table 4.9).

KEY FINDING

Children adopted by their previous foster carers were substantially older at each of the key stages of the adoption process.

* The two sub-groups of mixed parentage children were contrasted on the following variables: gender: χ^2=1.197 df 1 p=0.274 n.s.; legal status at assessment: χ^2=1.937 df 1 p=0.164 n.s.; placement for sibling groups: χ^2=0.087 df 1 p=0.768 n.s.; developmental problems: χ^2=0.430 df 1 p=0.512 n.s.; congenital risks: χ^2=0.615 df 1 p=0.433 n.s.; health condition: χ^2=4.104 df 2 p=0.128 n.s.; physical abuse: χ^2=1.617 df 1 p=0.204 n.s.; sexual abuse: χ^2=5.204 df 1 p=0.023 n.s.

† Age at entry: analysis of variance, F=2.181 df 1 p=0.142 n.s.; Age of child at "best interest" decision: F=11.696 df 1 at p<0.01.

‡ Differences were statistically significant: χ^2=14.707 df 1 at p<0.01; Phi=0.347.

** N=1,759 children; information missing in 42 children.

†† In BAAF's preceding analysis of all the children leaving care for adoption during 1996, the estimated number of foster parents adopting a child was between 16 and 25 per cent of the overall sample. The preparatory phase of the Adoption survey provided a more reliable figure with an average of 16 per cent of all agency adoptions during 1998 being by former foster carers (see Ivaldi, 1998; 1999).

Note: Years:months. N=1,759 children; information missing in 42 children. Foster carer adoptions (N=232), other children in the sample (N=1,527)

For children adopted by foster carers, "placement" refers to the actual date when the foster placement became an adoptive placement following the decision by the agency panel that adoption was in the child's best interests.

Mean age of child (yrs:mths)	Type of adoption		ANOVA Statistics		
	Foster carer adoption	New adoptive family	F	df	Sig.
Entry into care	1:10	1:0	46.311	1	p<0.01
"Best interest" decision	4:4	2:3	150.041	1	p<0.01
Placement with adopters	5:0	2:10	141.075	1	p<0.01
Adoption order	6:3	4:0	119.440	1	p<0.01

Children adopted by their foster carers were on average 10 months older than the other children on admission into care, and 2 years 1 month older when the agency decided that adoption was in the child's best interest. In cases where foster placements had become adoptive placements, the children were already aged 5 years as opposed to a mean age of 2 years 10 months in the children placed with "new" adoptive families. These differences were of course reflected in the mean age of those children at the making of the adoption order.

Lastly, an examination of the differences according to the five main types of local authority derived for the purpose of the analysis showed no significant variation in the overall rate of foster carer adoptions.*

4.2.4 Interagency placement and the role of the voluntary adoption agencies

The survey collected data from local authorities about the placement arrangements made with other agencies engaged in adoption activity and providing adoption services. In some cases it was the need to place particular children outside the geographical area of the relevant authority which probably led to inter-agency arrangements. In over a third (37 per cent) of the children adopted during 1998/99, the relevant agency had indicated the need to secure an adoptive placement outside the area or town.

There are also organisational constraints which explain why local authorities may decide to use external resources. The rationale for those pooling arrangements has been illustrated in recent research. In particular, the emphasis was placed on the imbalance between the availability of potential adopters and children requiring adoption in particular authorities, some agencies being found to have a 'surplus' of prospective adoptive families (Lowe and Murch, 1999).†

Placement of children through external agencies

The structure of the data helped identify specific cases where the agencies in the sample had to go to other local authorities or voluntary adoption societies to find suitable adopters for their children. Details are summarised in Table 4.10 below.

---

* χ^2=8.732 df 4 p=0.068 n.s. (N=1,759 children).

† Details of agency partnership and links with independent service user groups were examined in the preparatory phase of the survey. Over two thirds (68 per cent) of the responding authorities had a policy regarding the use of inter-agency placement. More than half (56 per cent) of the respondents were members of a local or regional consortium. In contrast, only very few local authorities were found to have a service agreement with the local voluntary sector for baby placement work (6 per cent). The corresponding figure for other adoption placement work with voluntary agencies was 16 per cent (see Ivaldi, 1999).

Adopters' recruiting agency	N	%
Same local authority	**1318**	**73**
Same agency	1252	69
New unitary after LGR	66	4
Other local authority	**191**	**11**
In England	175	10
In Scotland & Wales	16	1
Voluntary adoption agency	**292**	**16**
All children	**1,801**	**100**

Table 4.10

Interagency placements and the role of the voluntary adoption agencies

Note: N=all 1,801 children in the sample

In nearly three-quarters (73 per cent) of the children, local authorities had utilised their internal resources and found a match from within their own pool of approved adopters. Inter-agency placements involving another local authority accounted for 11 per cent of the cases, most (92 per cent) of which were located in England. Lastly, local authorities had looked to a voluntary organisation for a match in 16 per cent of the children.*

Variation in agency practice

One interesting finding was that the extent of interagency arrangements regarding adoption for looked after children varied significantly according to the type of local authority (see Figure 4.6).[†]

The use of external placing agencies was a distinctive feature of the inner London boroughs: the latter had worked in partnership with other adoption agencies in 44 per cent of their adoptions. This compared with 40, 35 and 31 per cent in the outer London area, new unitary authorities and metropolitan districts respectively. In contrast, only 12 per cent of the adoptions arranged by shire county social services had involved external resources.

KEY FINDING

In nearly three quarters of the children, local authorities had found a match from within their own pool of approved adopters.

KEY FINDING

Inter-agency placements involving another local authority accounted for 11 per cent of the cases.

KEY FINDING

Local authorities had found adopters through a voluntary organisation for 16 per cent of the children.

KEY FINDING

The use of external placing agencies was a distinctive feature of the inner London boroughs (44 per cent of their adoptions).

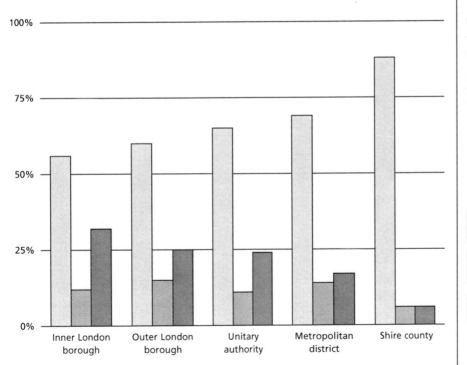

Figure 4.6

The extent of interagency placement by type of authority

Percentages of children within each type of local authority (N=1,801 children)

 Placed within local authority

Placed by another local authority

Placed by a voluntary adoption agency

* Applied to the whole cohort of the 2,200 children who left care for adoption during 1998/99, the above figure would produce a total of about 350 looked after children for whom suitable adopters were found by agencies in the voluntary sector.

† χ^2=120.951 df 8 p<0.01; Cramer's V=0.183

Interagency placements involving organisations in the voluntary sector were more frequent in London (32 and 25 per cent in the inner and outer boroughs respectively) and the unitary authorities of the sample (24 per cent).

The children's characteristics

Previous research has concentrated on the specific contribution by the voluntary sector to the adoption of looked after children. Voluntary adoption agencies are generally operating on a smaller scale, have specialised fieldworkers and tend to concentrate on finding adoptive families for particular categories of children. Main research findings suggest that the voluntary agencies are likely to be involved with the placement of older children with more complex care histories and special needs for whom it has proved difficult to find an adoptive family (Fratter *et al*, 1991, p.13; SSI, 1999, p.3; Ivaldi, 2000).

The adoption survey enabled comparison between the voluntary sector and statutory agencies in respect of the children adopted during 1998/99. However, there are differences between voluntary agencies and generalisations about the voluntary sector can be misleading, particularly if differences are to be analysed in terms of the respective merits of each sector.

The data confirmed that the children referred to external agencies for placement differed significantly from those placed by the relevant social

Table 4.11

Inter-agency placements and the profile of the children

Note: Children were grouped into 3 main categories: placed by the same authority, placed by another local authority and placed through a voluntary adoption agency. Percentages within each of these categories. * "Black" refers to African-Caribbean, African and Asian. ** Records of "possible" and "definite" sexual abuse were grouped together in order to avoid small counts

	Children placed			Chi-Square Statistics			
	Within local authority	By another local authority	By a voluntary adoption agency	χ^2	df	Sig.	Cramer's V
Gender							
% of boys	50	51	52	0.257	2	0.880	n.s.
Ethnicity							
% white	93	78	87	59.607	4	p<0.01	0.129
% black*	5	19	8				
% mixed parentage	2	3	5				
Legal status at assessment							
% voluntary agreement	24	24	11	23.100	2	p<0.01	0.113
% care, freeing orders	76	76	89				
Placement of sibling groups							
% placed with sibling(s)	34	32	51	31.931	2	p<0.01	0.133
% placed individually	66	68	49				
Special needs							
% developmental	15	21	22	11.509	2	p<0.01	0.080
% congenital risks	18	15	20	2.096	2	0.351	n.s.
Health problems							
% moderate	10	10	11	2.083	4	0.721	n.s.
% serious	5	6	6				
Abuse							
% physically abused	6	3	7	3.084	2	0.214	n.s.
% sexually abused**	4	1	4	2.824	2	0.260	n.s.
Placement history							
% single placement	38	44	32	16.371	6	p<0.01	0.067
% no return home	80	82	72	14.314	4	p<0.01	0.063

services department. One important area of difference was that of ethnicity, with children placed by other local authorities and voluntary adoption agencies being more likely to come from a minority ethnic background (22 and 13 per cent respectively against only 7 per cent of the children placed within the authority).

Children referred to the voluntary sector also had a very specific profile in terms of their legal status at the time of assessment and the extent to which placements were required for groups of siblings. Beginning with legal status, nearly nine in ten (89 per cent) of the children placed by voluntary agencies were looked after under care orders as opposed to three-quarters (76 per cent) of those placed by local authorities.

While two-thirds (68 per cent) of the local authority children had been adopted individually, it was only the case in half (49 per cent) of those referred to voluntary agencies.

Looking at the above differences in terms of the main groupings of children helped identify some important findings. Differences were mostly found in the contribution made by the voluntary sector in achieving placement for minority ethnic children, children under care orders, and those placed as part of a sibling group.

Table 4.12 contains the same information as that presented in Table 4.11 with percentages calculated in relation to these significant characteristics of the children. Relevant statistics were of course similar to those summarised in Table 4.11 and therefore were not duplicated in Table 4.12 below.

Of particular significance was that 29 per cent of the mixed parentage children had been placed through another local authority, while, for black children, adopters had been recruited by voluntary agencies in 28 per cent of the cases. The contribution by the voluntary sector was also evident in the children subject to compulsory care proceedings: of these children, 18 per

KEY FINDING

Children placed by other agencies were more likely to come from a minority ethnic background: 22 and 13 per cent respectively against only 7 per cent in the children placed within the authority.

KEY FINDING

Nearly nine in ten of the children placed by voluntary agencies were looked after under care orders as opposed to three quarters of those placed by local authorities.

KEY FINDING

Two thirds (68 per cent) of the local authority children had been adopted individually; it was only the case in half of those referred to voluntary agencies.

	Within local authority	By another local authority	By a voluntary adoption agency	Total
Ethnicity				
White	75	9	16	100
Black*	52	29	19	100
Mixed parentage	61	11	28	100
Legal status at assessment				
Voluntary agreement	80	12	8	100
Care, freeing orders	71	10	18	100
Placement for sibling groups				
Placed with sibling(s)	68	9	23	100
Placed individually	76	11	13	100

Table 4.12

The extent of inter-agency placement according to ethnicity, legal status and the number of children placed for adoption

Note: N=1,801 children. Percentages within groups of children. * "Black" refers to African-Caribbean, African and Asian

KEY FINDING

29 per cent of the mixed-parentage children had been placed through another local authority; for black children, adopters had been recruited by voluntary agencies in 28 per cent of the cases.

cent had been placed through voluntary agencies, as opposed to 8 per cent of those looked after under voluntary agreements. Lastly, nearly a quarter (23 per cent) of all the children adopted with birth sibling(s) had been provided with placement by voluntary agencies (against 13 per cent of the children placed individually).

There were also significant differences in the average ages of the children

KEY FINDING

Nearly a quarter of all the children adopted with birth sibling(s) had been provided with placement by voluntary agencies, against 13 per cent of the children placed individually.

placed through the voluntary sector. As suggested in Table 4.13, local authorities tended to place the youngest children within their own resources while referring older children to external agencies. Significant differences in mean ages of the children were found at each of the key phases of the process, with children referred to the voluntary sector being consistently older than those placed by local authorities.

The voluntary adoption agency children were for instance aged on average 3 years at time of "best interest" decision compared with 2 years 8 months for those referred to other local authorities and 2 years 5 months for those placed by their relevant authority. The contrast was striking when age at

Table 4.13

Inter-agency placements and the age profile of the children at the various stages of the adoption process

Note: Years:months. Children were grouped into 3 main categories: placed by the same authority, placed by another local authority and placed through a voluntary adoption agency (N=1,783 children, missing information in 18 cases)

	Children placed			ANOVA Statistics		
	Within local authority	By another local authority	By a Voluntary Adoption Agency	F	df	Sig.
Entry into care	1:0	1:4	1:4	7.160	2	p<0.01
"Best interest" decision	2:5	2:8	3:0	7.046	2	p<0.01
Placement with adopters	2:11	3:4	3:10	14.300	2	p<0.01
Adoption order	4:0	4:5	5:3	20.383	2	p<0.01

KEY FINDING

Children referred to the voluntary sector were consistently older than those placed by local authorities.

placement was considered: there was a difference of 11 months between the children placed within the local authority and those referred to a voluntary agency. The comparable figure for the average gap in age at adoption was 1 year 3 months.

Diversity of contribution by the voluntary sector

As discussed in the introduction to this section, there are important differences between voluntary agencies in terms of their size and the population they serve, which make it difficult to generalise about the voluntary sector as a whole. Voluntary adoption agencies remain a diverse group ranging from large national organisations to small local bodies.

Of particular relevance to the present part of the analysis was the agency's religious affiliation, which still represents a significant thread across the voluntary sector.*

Were there important dissimilarities in the profile of children referred for adoption to the secular, Catholic and Church of England organisations during 1998/99?

Comparing data on the children's characteristics for the above types of voluntary agencies revealed some variation. Here, the focus is exclusively on the subset of 292 children placed by adoption societies to allow investigation of the specific contribution made to the adoption of the 1998/99 cohort by each broad type of organisation in the voluntary sector. It must be noted that the analysis does not include cases of direct referrals of children who were not looked after by local authorities and would therefore not be included in the present sample of "agency" adoptions.

---

* The voluntary organisations which had provided adoptive placements for some of the children in the sample were clustered into 3 main categories: secular, Catholic and Church of England agencies.

In most cases, the comparison between categories of voluntary agency showed no significant differences in the actual profile of looked after children placed by these agencies on behalf of local authorities. This was true, for instance, for the balance of gender and the legal status of the children. Similarly, there was no clear indication of any substantial variation in the proportions of children listed with developmental, congenital and health problems.*

We did, however, find some empirical evidence of a specific contribution by some agencies within the voluntary sector in relation to the children's ethnicity and the extent of placement for sibling groups. With regard to the latter dimension, it was interesting to note that children placed with one or more birth siblings were significantly under-represented in the Catholic voluntaries of the sample: 65 per cent of the children placed by the Catholic agencies had been placed alone, whilst 60 and 58 per cent of those placed by the secular and Church of England societies respectively were part of a sibling group.[†]

Another noticeable set of findings related to the child's ethnic origin. Children placed by the secular agencies of the sample were more likely to be of minority ethnic background: nearly a quarter (24 per cent) of the children placed by secular voluntaries were of minority ethnic origin, which compared with only 5 and 2 per cent of those placed by the Catholic and Church of England agencies respectively (see Figure 4.7).[‡]

This was reflected in the extent to which relevant local authorities had expressed the need for the child to be linked with adopters of a similar ethnic background. The proportion of children for whom the agency was seeking ethnic matching was notably higher in cases where adoption had been arranged by secular voluntaries (40 per cent). The comparable figures

KEY FINDING

Children placed with one or more birth siblings were significantly under-represented in the Catholic voluntaries of the sample (35 per cent).

KEY FINDING

Children placed by the secular agencies of the sample were more likely to be of minority ethnic background: 24 per cent compared with only 5 and 2 per cent of those placed by the Catholic and Church of England agencies respectively.

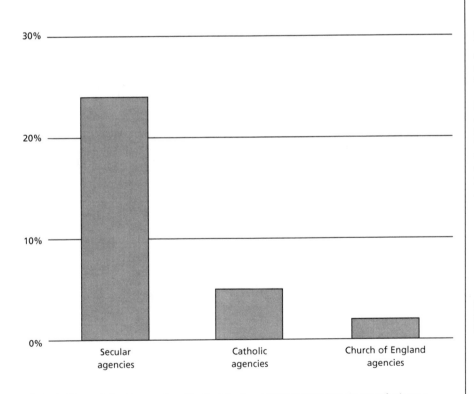

Figure 4.7

Adoption of children of a minority ethnic background by type of voluntary adoption agency

Note: * "Minority ethnic" refers here to African, African Caribbean and Asian, as well as children of mixed parentage. Voluntary agencies were clustered into three main categories. Percentages within each type of agency. N=292 looked after children placed for adoption by voluntary agencies during 1998/99 on behalf of local authorities.

per cent of minority ethnic* children placed by voluntary adoption agencies

* No statistically significant relationships were found for the following variables in relation to the type of voluntary adoption agency: gender: $\chi^2=5.553$ df 2 p=0.062 n.s.; legal status at time of approval: $\chi^2=1.333$ df 2 p=0.513 n.s.; developmental problems: $\chi^2=4.249$ df 2 p=0.120 n.s.; needs arising from heredity: $\chi^2=4.622$ df 2 p=0.099 n.s.; health problems: $\chi^2=12.805$ df 4 p=0.012 n.s.; physical abuse: $\chi^2=5.580$ df 2 p=0.061 n.s.; sexual abuse: $\chi^2=1.840$ df 4 p=0.765 n.s. N=292 looked after children placed for adoption by voluntary agencies during 1998/99 on behalf of local authorities.

† $\chi^2=16.653$ df 2 at p<0.01; Cramer's V=0.239 (N=292).

‡ $\chi^2=27.922$ df 4 at p<0.01; Cramer's V=0.219 (N=292).

Figure 4.8

Adoptions of looked after children arranged by voluntary adoption agencies: religious denomination of child by type of agency

Note: N=170 children placed by voluntary adoption agencies and for whom religious affiliation had been recorded. The small number of children of another Protestant (Free-Church) or non-Christian (essentially Muslim) denomination were removed from calculation.

per cent of children with no religion

per cent of Church of England children

per cent of Catholic children

were 21 and 28 per cent in the children placed by Catholic and Church of England voluntaries respectively.*

Not surprisingly, there was a significant pattern of association between the children's religious denomination and the type of voluntary organisation to which they had been referred for adoption (see Figure 4.8).[†]

Children with no particular religious affiliation were more frequently placed by the secular agencies of the study: 52 per cent of the children placed by secular agencies had no religion; 60 per cent of the children placed by

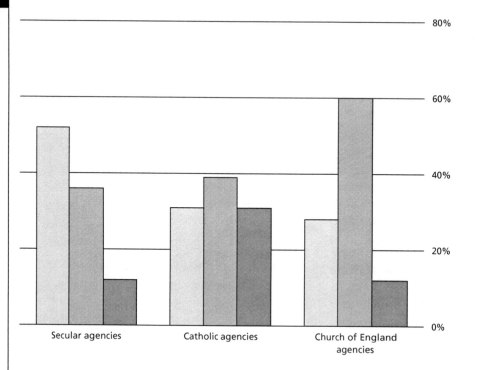

Church of England agencies were of a similar religious denomination. Less expected was perhaps the religious profile in the Catholic agencies, which showed no significant over-representation of Catholic children and each of the three groups were represented in equal proportions.

The need to find adopters of a similar religious denomination did not appear to influence the local authority's selection of a particular type of voluntary agency for religious matching. There was indeed very little variation when contrasting proportions of children listed with "same religion" requirements across the three main categories of voluntary organisations in the sample.[‡]

It should be remembered that the above findings are only relevant to the group of looked after children placed for adoption by voluntary adoption agencies on behalf of local authorities. Patterns of association between the child's religious needs and the type of agency preferred for adoptive placement may prove significantly different when considering cases of direct referrals made by birth parents for young infants outside the care of social services departments.

* χ^2=10.772 df 2 at p<0.01; Cramer's V=0.192 (N=292).

† χ^2=15.595 df 4 at p<0.01; Cramer's V=0.214. The small number of children of another Protestant (Free Church) or non-Christian denomination were removed from calculation (N=170 children placed by voluntary adoption agencies and for whom religious affiliation had been recorded).

‡ χ^2=0.967 df 2 p=0.617 n.s. (N=292 children placed by voluntary adoption agencies).

4.2.5 Birth parents' attitudes towards adoption

One last area of interest was that of the birth parents' response to the adoption plan for their children. Again, it is essential to stress that the statistics presented in this section are only relevant to the assessment phase of the whole process. The design of the survey did not allow the recording of subsequent changes in the birth parents' attitude towards adoption.

As shown in Table 4.14, the birth mother's agreement or disagreement to the adoption plan was recorded in the vast majority (92 per cent) of the children adopted during 1998/99. Of these, the proportion of cases where the birth mother did not agree to the plan amounted to 58 per cent. In contrast, the birth father's attitude towards adoption was known in half (55 per cent) of the cases, with a similar proportion (58 per cent) of fathers disagreeing with the decision made by the agency to seek adoption for the children.

KEY FINDING

58 per cent of the birth mothers did not agree to the plan for adoption.

KEY FINDING

The birth father's attitude towards adoption was known in half of the cases, with a similar proportion (58 per cent) of fathers disagreeing with the decision made by the agency to seek adoption.

Table 4.14

Birth parents' agreement to adoption for their child(ren)

Note: Percentage of all children (N=1,801). *As recorded on assessment material at time of referral of child for adoption.

Parental agreement to adoption*	Birth mother			Birth father		
	N	per cent of all cases	per cent of cases where parental agreement was recorded	N	per cent of all cases	per cent of cases where parental agreement was recorded
Did not agree to the plan	962	53	58	570	32	58
Did agree to the plan	703	39	42	416	23	42
Total valid responses	1,665	92	100	985	55	100
Not specified on form	136	8		816	45	
TOTAL	1,801	100		1,801	100	

A total of 53 per cent of children had been approved for adoption with both parents contesting the plan, while for another 29 per cent of the children, both parents had accepted the decision made by the relevant local authority. Cases of birth parents presenting opposite views over the adoption plan accounted for the remaining 18 per cent of the children sample, of which two-thirds were cases where the birth father had approved the plan while the mother was against it.*

Concentrating on whether the birth mother had agreed to the plan showed substantial differences in the children's characteristics in terms of legal status, age at entry and best interest decision, and the extent of placement for sibling groups. The most significant differences are summarised in Table 4.15.

Not surprisingly, there was a strong relationship between the birth mother's approval of adoption and the legal status of child at time of assessment: in the overwhelming majority (93 per cent) of the children accommodated under voluntary agreements, there was an indication that the birth mother had agreed to the adoption plan. This compared with only 28 per cent in the children looked after under compulsory care proceedings.

Cases where the birth mother had not contested the agency decision to pursue adoption for the particular child were more frequent in the children

KEY FINDING

A total of 53 per cent of children had been approved for adoption with both parents contesting the plan.

KEY FINDING

In the overwhelming majority (93 per cent) of the children accommodated voluntarily, the birth mother had agreed to the adoption plan, as opposed to 28 per cent of the children looked after under compulsory care proceedings.

---

* These figures refer only to the 953 children of the sample for whom agreement or disagreement by both parents had been recorded on the assessment form.

Table 4.15

Birth mother's agreement to adoption and the profile of the children

Note: N=1,665; missing data in 136 children. Percentages of birth mother's agreement within each category of children

	Birth mother agreement			Chi-Square Statistics			
	% did not agree	% did agree to the plan	Total	χ²	df	Sig.	Cramer's V
Legal status at assessment							
care order	72	28	100	492.817	1	p<0.01	0.544
voluntary agreement	7	93	100				
Placement for sibling groups							
placed individually	50	50	100	66.417	1	p<0.01	0.200
placed with sibling(s)	71	29	100				
Age at entry into care							
under 1 month	47	53	100	50.155	3	p<0.01	0.174
1–12 months	63	37	100				
1–5 years	66	34	100				
5 years and over	64	36	100				
Age at "best interest"							
under 6 months	29	71	100	139.155	4	p<0.01	0.291
6–12 months	65	35	100				
12–30 months	67	33	100				
30 months–5 years	67	33	100				
5 years and over	56	44	100				

KEY FINDING

Cases where the birth mother had not contested the agency decision were more frequent in the children placed alone: 50 per cent as opposed to 29 per cent in the children placed with siblings.

KEY FINDING

Proportions of adoption cases where birth mothers had approved the plan were higher in the outer areas of London (55 per cent) and shire counties (47 per cent).

placed alone (50 per cent as opposed to 29 per cent in the children placed with siblings). Birth mother approval to adoption was also more likely to have been reached in relation to the very young infants of the sample aged under 1 month at entry (53 per cent) and under 6 months at time of "best interest" decision (71 per cent).

Lastly, there was some evidence of a variation in the overall rate of agreement by birth mothers across the main types of local authorities in the sample (see Figure 4.9). Although statistically significant, these differences were less graphic than those observed in the preceding part of the analysis concerning the children's profile in terms of legal proceedings, age, and the number of children placed for adoption.*

Figure 4.9

Birth mother's agreement to adoption across main types of local authority

Note: N=1,665 missing data in 136 children. Percentages of birth mother's agreement within each category of agency.

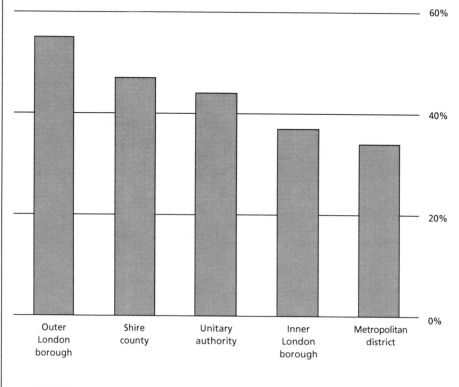

* χ²=29.245 df 4 at p<0.01; Cramer's V=0.132.

Proportions of adoption cases where birth mothers had approved the plan were higher in the Outer areas of London (55 per cent) and shire counties (47 per cent). In contrast, key workers in both the metropolitan districts and inner London boroughs had faced birth mother disagreement with the adoption plan for nearly two-thirds of the children (66 and 63 per cent respectively).

References

Fratter, J Rowe, J Sapsford, D and Thoburn, J (1991) *Permanent Family Placement: A decade of experience*, London: BAAF.

Ivaldi, G (1998) *Children Adopted from Care: An examination of agency adoptions in England – 1996*, London: BAAF.

Ivaldi, G (1999) *BAAF Adoption Survey 1998/99: Report on the preparatory phase – records, management and policy*, London: BAAF.

Ivaldi, G (2000) *Children and Families in the Voluntary Sector: An overview of child placement and adoption work by the voluntary adoption agencies in England 1994-98*, London: BAAF.

Lowe, N Murch, M Borkowski, M Weaver, A Beckford, V with Thomas, C (1999) *Supporting Adoption: Reframing the Approach*, London: BAAF.

Parker, R (1999) *Adoption Now: Messages from Research*, Chichester: John Wiley & Sons.

Social Services Inspectorate, Department of Health (1999) *Meeting the Challenges of Changes in Adoption – Inspection of Voluntary Adoption Agencies*, CI(99)7.

The timing of adoption procedures

So far, we have explored some important patterns of adoption for looked after children, mainly by looking at the characteristics of the children, their placement history and the relationship between the two. Because the adoption process spans several months or years, another crucial area of concern to be tackled is the length of time that elapsed between each stage of the process. In this chapter, the focus is on the time-scales of the adoption pathway out of care, particularly in relation to possible factors which might influence the delays that may occur in securing adoptive placements.

The adoption survey was designed to allow a comprehensive investigation of the time-scales in local authority adoption during 1998/99, not only in terms of the overall duration of care before adoption was finalised but also in relation to some of the key segments of the whole process. Issues relating to time-scales in the different phases are dealt with in this part of the analysis together with the assessment of potential causes of delay.

5.1 Overview

Before turning to the analysis of possible delay, it is important to provide the reader with an overview of the children's mean duration of care during the main sequences of leaving care through to adoption (see all relevant definitions in Chapter 4). Although issues in relation to post-adoption support and practice by local authorities are of the utmost importance, these were clearly outside the scope of this survey.

Average waiting phases are considered descriptively in Figure 5.1 below.

Figure 5.1

The "pace" of the adoption process

Note: Average durations between stages in the adoption process, and average age at each stage (years:months). Data were missing for 18 children of the sample (N=1,783)

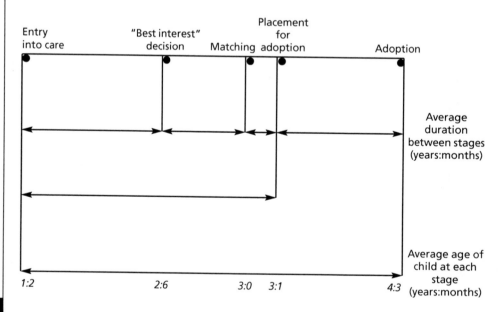

KEY FINDING

The mean overall duration of care was 3 years and 1 month in all the children.

The mean overall duration of care was 3 years 1 month in all the children, ranging from a minimum of 5 months up to 17 years 4 months.*

* By "duration of care" we refer to the total length of time which has elapsed between date of first admission to care and the actual date of adoption, that is, the making of the adoption order by the court. By contrast, in 1996, the mean length of time in care was 3 years 8 months for all the adopted children, with a broad range from 13 weeks to 17 years 9 months, and a standard deviation of 2 years 8 months.

On average, the best interest decision had been made within 1 year 4 months after the child started to be looked after by the relevant local authority, while it took another 7 months before placement with adopters was achieved. From the actual range in the period of waiting prior to placement, it was also clear that some children in the sample had spent several years in care before being linked with adopters. The mean length of time between placement and adoption was 14 months, with a range from 3 months to about 10 years (9 years 8 months).

5.2 Factors of delay

Periods of waiting which children may encounter during their time in care are the focus of major concern and criticism. The potential impact of the child's characteristics, needs and early experiences on the subsequent development of adoption proceedings and the variations in the timespan between the different stages of the process were considered.

Most of these variables did exert an influence on the period of waiting between "best interest" decision and placement with adopters, although only some of the variables accounted for the variation in the child's duration of care prior to being approved for adoption or, considering the other end of the spectrum, the time waiting for adoption following placement with adopters.*

It was equally important to recognise the significance of existing patterns of relationships among the factors considered for the analysis. Important background characteristics of the children such as age, ethnicity or legal proceedings may combine or cancel out their effects on the time taken for each phase of the process. As we shall see, some variables were not relevant to all the stages of the adoption process. These questions are examined in turn in the following sections.

5.2.1 Identifying children for adoption

We shall start by looking at the period between entry into the public care system and the decision by the agency to approve the child for adoption. Some factors affecting delays experienced by the children are found in the earlier stages of their care history, and patterns of entry into care tend to impact on the subsequent development of the children's career within the system. The following analyses are only relevant to the cohort of children who were successfully adopted out of care during 1998/99.

Preliminary analysis of variance for the mean duration of time in care prior to "best interest" decision pointed to differences according to three main variables: legal status, age at entry, and whether the child was to be placed subsequently as part of a sibling group.†

In addition, we looked at the length of waiting time prior to being identified for adoption for the children who were initially placed with foster carers and were subsequently adopted by them. For these children, the duration of care before approval was twice as long as that of the other children, which called for further investigation of other aspects of the child's profile and history.‡

---

* Given that placement usually occurred soon after the match had been made between children and their new families, there was a case for concentrating on the point of placement. Examining children's duration of care between "best interest" decision and matching of child with adopters revealed no significant variation in the factors that were likely to exert an influence on the length of time between "best interest" and placement.

† All three variables were found to exert a significant influence on the length of time needed to identify children suitable for adoption. ANOVA statistics were as follows: age at entry: F=64.133 df 3 at p<0.01; legal status at time of assessment: F=57.516 df 1 at p<0.01; placement for sibling groups: F=40.400 df 1 at p<0.01.

‡ F=142.346 df 1 at p<0.01; % of explained variance = 7.5 per cent.

KEY FINDING

On average, the best interest decision had been made within 1 year 4 months after the child started to be looked after, and it took another 7 months before placement with adopters was achieved.

KEY FINDING

The mean length of time between placement and adoption was 14 months.

None of the other characteristics were found to exert a significant influence on the time of waiting between entry and approval for adoption.

It must be noted that the information concerning the child's legal status, placement with siblings, and adoption by foster carers relates to a later stage of the adoption process, namely, the point of approval for adoption. There may be important changes in the child's circumstances at the various stages of the process: for instance, a child placed with siblings may well have initially entered care alone. Similarly, the analysis reported in Chapter 3 showed that there had been a change in legal status between entry and approval from voluntary agreements to care orders for a substantial proportion of the adopted children.

Bearing this in mind, differences were assessed in the context of the existing patterns of covariation between the age, legal status and sibling group factors.*

Performing an analysis of variance revealed that age on entry into care retained its main effect when controlling for the other two characteristics of the children. There was, however, some variation in the extent to which age at entry impacted on the length of time that elapsed in the course of identifying children for adoption.

Age at entry and legal procedures

The first important dimension associated with the age profile was that of the child's legal status. In light of what has been said regarding patterns of entry into care, and their potential impact on the children's subsequent progress, it is important to stress again that the information considered for the analysis refers to the child's legal status at the time of assessment for adoption and does not therefore provide any insight into the actual circumstances of the child when received into care.

Bearing this in mind, there were two different patterns according to the age on admission combined with legal procedures involved in looking after the child (see Figure 5.2). This suggested that the way in which local authorities had responded either to the situation leading to the child's entry into care, or subsequent changes to the child's circumstances during their time of being looked after, affected significantly the duration of care prior to approval for adoption.

KEY FINDING

For the children looked after under section 20 there was a strong linear increase in the average duration of time in care prior to 'best interest' decision across age groups.

Figure 5.2

Average time between entry into care and "best interest" decision: the interaction of age on admission and legal status

Note: Years. N=1,783 children (information was missing in 18 cases). Legal status at time of assessment

Section 20

Care order

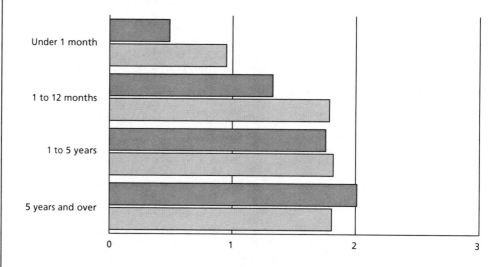

* As evidenced by previous exploration of the data in this study, there were strong relationships between age, legal status and the extent of placement for sibling groups. Chi-Square statistics were as follows: legal status * sibling group (χ^2=83.470 df 1 p<0.01; Cramer's V=0.215); legal status * age at entry (χ^2=156.267 df 3 p<0.01; Cramer's V=0.295) ; age at entry * sibling group (χ^2=308.028 df 3 p<0.01; Cramer's V=0.414).

For the subset of children looked after under voluntary agreements, there was a strong linear increase in the average duration of time in care prior to agency "best interest" decision across age groups. The older the children were at entry, the more likely they were to have longer duration of care prior to approval for adoption.*

There was little empirical evidence of such a linear relationship in the children looked after under care orders. Only babies aged under 1 month on entry had spent less time in care prior to being approved for adoption: on average it took 11 months to identify these very young infants as suitable for adoptive placement compared with approximately 1 year 10 months for the rest of the children.†

The impact of legal proceedings was clearly restricted to the group of infants aged under 1 year on entry into care. For the infants under one month at entry and looked after voluntarily, the mean time of care before the agency decided to proceed with adoption was 6 months. This compared with an average of 11 months for those subjected to compulsory orders. A similar pattern was found in the 1–12 months age band, with a difference of about 5 months according to the child's legal status.‡

This difference was not evident for any of the older children in the sample, and emphasised the specific profile of babies voluntarily relinquished for adoption by their birth parents. In respect of these very young infants, it should be noted, for instance, that birth mothers had agreed to adoption in 92 per cent of the cases. Moreover, 96 per cent of those babies were subsequently placed individually.

For the latter group of infants admitted into care under 1 month of age, looked after under section 20 and placed alone, the ethnic background of child impacted significantly on the time taken from entry to approval for adoption – this was different to the impact of ethnic background on the wider sample where it was not significant to the length of wait. Both the white and mixed parentage infants in that particular category had waited 5-and-a-half months before being approved for adoption, as opposed to an average of one year for the black infants.**

Age at entry and placement for sibling groups

Another interesting finding was that of the combined effect of age at entry and the extent of placement for sibling groups.††

Differences between children placed singly and those placed as part of a sibling group were of a lower magnitude among the very young babies of the sample, with a gap of about 2 months between the infants placed alone and those adopted with one or more siblings. As indicated in Figure 5.3, this gap was further accentuated in the 1–12 months age group where children placed individually were found to have a significantly shorter duration of care prior to approval for adoption.‡‡

| 5 | Timing of procedures |

KEY FINDING

In the children looked after under care orders, only babies aged under 1 month on admission had spent less time in care prior to being approved for adoption: 11 months on average compared with approximately 1 year and 10 months for the rest of the children.

KEY FINDING

For the group of relinquished singletons under 1 month, the ethnic background impacted significantly on the time taken from entry to identification for adoption: the white and mixed parentage infants had waited 5 and a half months, as opposed to one year for the black infants.

KEY FINDING

Differences between children placed alone and those placed as part of a sibling group were of a low magnitude amongst the very young babies with a gap of about 2 months. In the 1-12 months age group, children placed individually had a significantly shorter duration of care prior to being identified for adoption.

---

* Pearson's $r=0.466$ significant at $p<0.01$, 2-tailed; both variables expressed in number of days; N=386 children looked after under section 20.

† Post hoc pairwise multiple comparisons with Bonferroni test at the 1 per cent level of significance. It is also interesting to note that there was no strong correlation between age at entry and time elapsed between admission and the "best interest" decision (Pearson's $r=0.204$ significant at $p<0.01$, 2-tailed; both variables expressed in number of days; N=1,397 children looked after under care orders).

‡ These differences were statistically significant at the 0.01 level (post hoc pairwise multiple comparisons with Bonferroni test).

** $F=4.812$ df 2 at $p<0.01$; N=241 infants under 1 month looked after under a voluntary agreement and placed for adoption alone. "Black" refers to African, African-Caribbean and Asian.

†† Simple factorial analysis of variance, 2-way interaction between age at entry and placement for sibling groups: $F=9.002$ df 3 at $p<0.01$.

‡‡ All differences statistically significant at the 0.01 level (post hoc pairwise multiple comparisons with Bonferroni test).

Figure 5.3

Time between entry into care and "best interest" decision: the interaction of age on admission and placement for sibling groups

Note: Years. N=1,783 children (information was missing in 18 cases).

Children placed individually

Children placed with sibling(s)

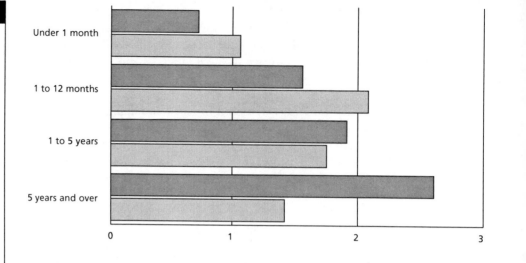

By contrast, older children entering care over the age of 1 year and subsequently placed with one or more siblings waited a shorter time before the "best interest" decision was made by the relevant local authority. This was particularly true of the children aged 5 years and over on entry: in that age band, children placed as part of a sibling group had waited on average 1 year 5 months to be approved for adoption. The comparable figure for children placed singly was 2 years 7 months.*

This gap called for further exploration of the children's characteristics. There was some evidence that the single children aged 5 and over on entry were more likely to have special needs, in terms of their health condition, developmental difficulties, and history of abuse and neglect. Unfortunately the size of the group of older children adopted alone in the sample was too small to test the statistical significance of these differences.

Adoption by foster carer(s)

"Delay" in adoption proceedings may be less significant in cases where the children were adopted by foster carers. The survey did not permit any assessment of the reasons why foster placements had been turned into adoptive ones, and whether it was the foster parents or the relevant local authority who called for the change in the type of stable placement secured for the particular child. However, it can be assumed that the vast majority of those placements started with no particular view about adoption.

As indicated earlier, there was a wide variation in the length of time that elapsed between entry into care and the decision that the child should be considered for adoption according to whether the child was subsequently adopted by their foster carers. In cases of carers adopting their foster child(ren), the mean duration of care prior to approval was as high as 2 years 6 months, with a maximum of about 17 years. This compared with an average of 1 year 3 months in the rest of the sample.

This pattern was found to be very consistent across all subsets of children classified according to gender, ethnicity, legal status and the number of children placed with adopters. Regardless of any of the above characteristics, children adopted by their foster carers had consistently spent a longer time in care before the need for an adoptive placement was identified.†

KEY FINDING

In cases of carers adopting their foster child(ren), the mean duration of care prior to identification for adoption was 2 years 6 months, compared with an average of 1 year 3 months in the rest of the sample.

KEY FINDING

Regardless of any other characteristics, children adopted by their foster carers had consistently spent a longer time in care before the need for an adoptive placement was identified.

KEY FINDING

Mixed parentage children placed with a "new" adoptive family had waited for 1 year 3 months, as opposed to 4 years 1 month for those adopted by their foster carers.

* Statistically significant at the 0.01 level.

† The impact of foster carer adoption was controlled for gender, ethnicity, legal status and the number of children placed for adoption. All ANOVA statistics were significant at the 0.01 level, with the exception of the black children (African, African-Caribbean and Asian), mainly due to the small size of the sample of foster carer adoptions in that particular group ($F=0.489$ df 1 $p=0.488$ n.s.). Relevant values of F [df=1 at $p<0.01$] were as follows (N=1,759 missing data in 42 children): Boys: $F=68.930$; Girls: $F=74.100$; White: $F=128.996$; Mixed parentage: $F=30.458$; Section 20: $F=24.081$; Care order: $F=109.080$; Single child: $F=123.412$; Placed with sibling(s): $F=26.387$.

Differences were particularly striking for the mixed parentage children, with an average of 1 year 3 months before approval for the children placed with a "new" adoptive family, as opposed to 4 years 1 month for those adopted by their foster carers.

More importantly, perhaps, the impact of foster carer adoptions was apparent across all age bands and proved statistically robust when controlled for the age of child at entry into care.*

The combined effect of the two factors was of great relevance to the older children aged 5 years and over when received into care: in the latter, the average duration of care was as high as 3 years in cases where the adoptive parents were foster carers, against 1 year 5 months for the children placed for adoption with a new family.[†]

5.2.2 Identifying suitable adopters

The second main sequence of the adoption process starts with the approval of the child for adoption. Critical issues are the actual length of time that preceded placement with the adoptive family, and whether there may be children more difficult to place because of their individual profile, history or

5 Timing of procedures

KEY FINDING

The impact of foster carer adoptions was apparent across all age bands and proved statistically robust when controlled for the age of child at entry into care.

KEY FINDING

The combined effect of age and foster carer adoption was strong in the older children aged 5 years and over: a period of 3 years in cases where the adoptive parents were previous foster carers, against 1 year 5 months for the children placed for adoption with a new family.

Child's characteristics	From "best interest" decision to placement — Deviation from sample mean	ANOVA statistics — df	F	% of variance
Gender				
Male	+ 2 weeks	1	7.566	0.4
Ethnicity (3 groups)				
Mixed parentage	+ 8 weeks			
Black*	+ 5 months	2	14.071	1.6
Legal status (2 groups)				
Section 20	– 9 weeks	1	40.518	2.2
Developmental needs	+ 3 months	1	57.778	3.1
Health problems (3 groups)				
Moderate	+ 3 weeks			
Serious	+ 6 months	2	29.302	3.2
Physical abuse	+ 8 weeks	1	6.717	0.4
Poor parenting / neglect	+ 6 weeks	1	6.995	0.4
Placement of sibling group				
Child with sibling(s)	+ 4 weeks	1	15.532	0.9
Birth mother's agreement	– 5 weeks	1	23.437	1.4
Adoption by foster carer(s)	+6 weeks	1	7.501	0.4
Age at "best interest"				
Under 6 months	– 4 months	4	41.547	8.5
6–12 months	– 5 weeks			
12–30 months	–			
30 months-5 years	+ 9 weeks			
5 years and over	+ 3 months			

Table 5.1

Factors significantly associated with time taken to identify suitable adopters: main statistical effects and deviation from mean in the whole sample

Note: ANOVA statistics. All values of the F statistic significant at $p<0.01$. N=1,783 (information missing in 18 children).
* "Black" refers to African, African-Caribbean and Asian.

* ANOVA specifying "age on admission" as a covariate: age: F=39.545 df 1 at p<0.01; Foster carer adoption: F=139.853 df 1 at p<0.01 (N=1,759 missing data in 42 children).

[†] It is interesting to note that in the "5 years+" age group (N=73), the interaction between age and foster carer adoption explained a total of 26.2 per cent of the variance, that is a significant part of the variation in duration of care prior to approval for adoption.

family background. Analysis of variance showed a variety of characteristics that accounted for differences in time of finding suitable adopters for the children in need of a permanent substitute family (see Table 5.1).

What is demonstrated in Table 5.1 is the potential impact of a wide range of child's characteristics on significant deviation from mean in the sample. Considered separately, however, each of the above factors would fail to explain more than 8.5 per cent of the total variation in pre-placement time of care following approval for adoption.

At stake here is how these variables combine and act together to affect periods of waiting for placement. The relationships between factors such as the child's age, legal route to adoption or special needs are inevitably complex and make difficult any attempt to untangle the influence of each particular variable. The analysis in the following sections makes a tentative evaluation of significant interactions between those factors, bearing in mind that the role of other unidentified variables cannot be excluded and may contribute to explaining some of the variability in children's length of placement period.

The impact of age at time of making the "best interest" decision

KEY FINDING

Children approved for adoption at an older age were more likely to have longer duration of care prior to placement with adopters.

In examining first the potential for age at "best interest" decision affecting the overall length of time of being looked after between "best interest" decision and placement, we found significant differences between the children in the sample. Time before placement varied significantly according to the age of child at time of "best interest" decision. Significantly, children approved for adoption at an older age were more likely to have longer duration of care prior to being placed with adopters.*

KEY FINDING

The mean duration of time between "best interest" decision and placement was 3 months for babies approved before 6 months of age, compared with 10 months in the children who had been approved aged 5 and over.

At one extreme, the average duration of time between "best interest" decision and placement was 3 months for children approved before 6 months of age, while at the opposite end of the age spectrum the mean average was 10 months in the children who had been approved aged 5 and over (see Figure 5.4).

However, investigating differences between age bands suggested that infants aged 6 to 12 months had a very similar profile to that of the children within

Figure 5.4

Time between "best interest" decision and placement with adopters: the impact of age at approval for adoption

Note: Months. N=1,783 children (information was missing in 18 cases).

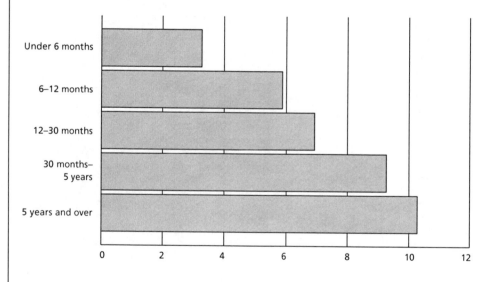

* For the purpose of the analysis, children were regrouped into 5 main categories of age at "best interest" decision: under 6 months, 6–12 months, 12–30 months, 30 months–5 years, 5 years and over. See Table 5.1 in the introduction of this section for details of relevant ANOVA statistics.

the 12–30 months age group in respect of their time of waiting for placement. Differences between the children aged 30 months–5 years and those falling into the 5 years and over age band were not statistically significant.*

The above relationship between age and the length of time from approval for adoption to placement with adopters held true when controlling for the rest of the variables considered for the analysis, including the main types of local authority looking after the children.†

Overall, the impact of age was apparent in all categories of children. This indicated that, although restricted to three broad categories, the age profile of child when approved for adoption was an important factor of the subsequent period of waiting for a suitable match with adopters.

Gender of child

Statistical differences in waiting time between approval and placement in terms of the child's gender proved significantly less robust across other groupings of children in the study. It should be stressed that the gender gap was of a low magnitude in the whole sample, and that, considered alone, whether the child was male or female made very little difference.‡

Comparing average duration of care prior to placement according to other potentially influential factors revealed that the child's gender was a significant factor in a limited number of cases only, and that the most important factor was the interaction of gender with other characteristics of the child.

Age at "best interest" decision was clearly a significant variable to be considered for the analysis, with differences between boys and girls being restricted to the group of children aged 30 months and over when approved for adoption. In the latter age band, boys had waited on average 11 months for placement as opposed to 8 months for the girls. Similar analysis of variance pointed to the absence of any significant impact of gender in all the younger children and infants of the sample.**

For older children, the gender gap was further accentuated when taking account of the presence of a child's siblings and special needs. Differences between boys and girls were particularly striking when considering the subset of children approved for adoption individually and aged 30 months and over. In these children, the gap between boys and girls was as large as 5 months.††

These differences were partly explained by the existing pattern of covariation between age at "best interest" decision and the child's special developmental

KEY FINDING

Infants aged 6 to 12 months had a very similar profile to that of the children within the 12–30 months age group in respect of their time of waiting for placement. Similarly, differences between the children aged 30 months–5 years and those aged 5 years+ were not statistically significant.

KEY FINDING

The impact of age was apparent in all categories of children.

KEY FINDING

Gender was a significant factor albeit restricted to the group of children aged 30 months and over when approved for adoption. In that age band, boys had waited on average 11 months for placement as opposed to 8 months for the girls.

KEY FINDING

Differences between boys and girls were particularly striking when considering the subset of children approved for adoption individually and aged 30 months and over. In those children, the gap between boys and girls was as high as 5 months.

* Post hoc pairwise multiple comparisons with Bonferroni test at the 1 per cent level of significance. Again, it is important to stress that there was no strong linear correlation between age at approval for adoption and the length of time between "best interest" decision and placement (Pearson's $r=0.225$ significant at $p<0.01$, 2-tailed; both variables expressed in number of days; N=1,783).

† Successive simple factorial analyses of variance were performed for age at "best interest" decision together with each of the following factors: gender, ethnicity (3 groups), legal status (2 groups), type of agency (5 categories), developmental needs, health problems (3 groups), physical abuse, poor parenting / neglect, placement of sibling group and birth mother's agreement to adoption. All F statistics for the main effect of age at "best interest" were found to be significant at the 0.01 level.

‡ A model based solely on gender of child would account for less than 0.5 per cent of the total variation in the length of time waiting for placement (see Table 5.1 in the introduction).

** Because the only significant differences related to age were found for three groups of children, the information was restricted to a comparison between infants under 6 months, children aged 6 to 30 months, and older children over 30 months at time of approval. ANOVA statistics for the impact of gender within these main categories of age were as follows: under 6 months ($F=0.026$ df 1 $p=0.872$ n.s.); 6–30 months ($F=0.636$ df 1 $p=0.425$ n.s.); 30 months and over ($F=9.683$ df 1 at $p<0.01$).

†† $F=15.876$ df 1 at $p<0.01$; N=296 children aged 30 months and over at time of "best interest" decision and placed for adoption individually.

needs (see Chapter 3). The analysis found empirical evidence of a similar gender gap in the group of children described as having developmental and/or learning difficulties.*

The following sections will address the issue of the child's special needs and how they may affect the process of placing looked after children for adoption.

Seeking adoptive placements for minority ethnic children

An important area of interest was the problems which local authorities may experience when seeking adoption placements for looked after children from a minority ethnic background. Examining children's duration of care prior to placement provided an opportunity to assess the impact of patterns of ethnic origin on the subsequent development of children's careers in the public care system.

The exploratory analysis of variance detailed in the preceding section pointed to important differences in terms of the child's ethnic origin, which were indicative of the relevance of clustering the children into three main categories of ethnic background.

Differences between ethnic groups in relation to time of waiting for placement were found to be significant across all categories of children classified according to age, gender, legal status, and placement of siblings.[†]

Controlling for other important characteristics of the children not only confirmed the variation between the white and minority ethnic children but also revealed two main patterns of interaction in respect of the length of time from approval for adoption to placement with adopters: first, the combined effect of ethnicity and age; second, the interaction between gender and ethnic origin of child.[‡]

The first of these two models is illustrated in Figure 5.5 below, which contains a breakdown of the child's ethnic origin according to age at "best interest" decision.

Figure 5.5

Time between "best interest" decision and placement with adopters: the interaction between ethnic origin and age at approval for adoption

Note: Months. N=1,783 children (information was missing in 18 cases). * "Black" refers to African, African-Caribbean and Asian.

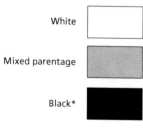

White

Mixed parentage

Black*

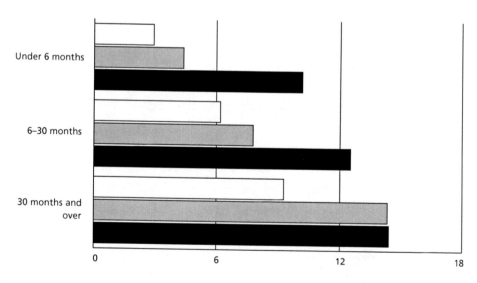

* Figures were very similar to those derived for older children. Within the particular category of children with developmental problems, boys had waited on average 12 months for placement, compared with 7 months for the girls (F= df 1 at p<0.01; N=298 children with developmental needs).

† In all the following parts of the analysis, one should exercise some caution when interpreting the findings for the relatively small number of African-Caribbean, Black African and Asian children in the 1998/99 cohort.

‡ Simple factorial analyses of variance. Statistically significant 2-way interactions: age*ethnicity: F=9.119 df 4 at p<0.01; gender*ethnicity: F=24.332 df 2 at p<0.01. Analysis of between-group variance pointed to other significant differences in the length of time spent in care between approval and placement according to legal status and the extent of placement for sibling groups, and thus yielded patterns consistent with those identified by previous analysis. However, these differences were mostly accounted for by the age factor and were below the level of statistical significance when specifying age as a covariate.

Both white and mixed parentage children aged under 30 months at time of approval for adoption shared relatively similar periods of waiting for placement, which were significantly shorter than those of black children in the relevant age groups.*

For instance, black infants under the age of 6 months had waited 10 months for placement as opposed to 3 and 4 months for white and mixed parentage infants respectively. In contrast, the combination of age and ethnicity in the older children approved aged 30 months and over led to a shorter wait for placement for white children alone (9 months on average), compared with 14 months for both black and mixed parentage children in that particular age band.

KEY FINDING

In the older children aged 30 months+, there was a shorter wait for placement for white children alone (9 months on average), compared with 14 months for both black and mixed parentage children.

Figure 5.6

Time between "best interest" decision and placement with adopters: the interaction between ethnic origin and gender of child

Note: Months. N=1,783 children (information was missing in 18 cases).
* "Black" refers to African, African-Caribbean and Asian.

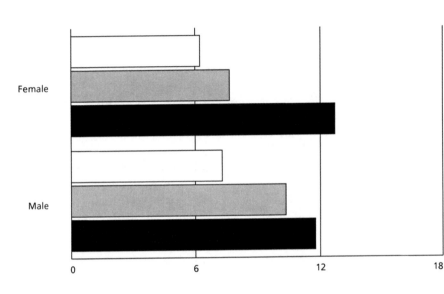

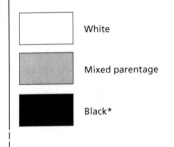

White

Mixed parentage

Black*

The structure of interaction between gender and ethnicity was very similar to that revealed in the above analysis and confirmed that the length of the pre-placement phase following approval for adoption was certainly associated with these two factors. The combined effect of gender and ethnicity on duration of time in care before placement is shown in Figure 5.6.

For the adopted girls, the differences were mostly between white and mixed parentage children, on the one hand, and black children. The former had waited on average between 6 and 8 months to be provided with an adoptive placement, compared with 12 months for the latter. Comparable figures for boys in the sample showed a different pattern, with white children having a significantly shorter duration of care prior to placement when compared with that of both the mixed parentage and black boys: 7 months as opposed to 10 and 12 months respectively.†

One important issue that remains outstanding in relation to ethnicity is that of the social composition of the population served by social services departments. Unfortunately, the samples of black and mixed parentage children were too small to assess with accuracy the impact of region, density of local authority population, or type of agency. Where the comparison was possible in terms of the main categories of authority in the study, the analysis revealed a very similar pattern of association, with minority ethnic children waiting longer on average before joining prospective adopters.‡

KEY FINDING

For the adopted girls, the differences were mostly between white and mixed parentage children, on the one hand, and black children. The former had waited on average between 6 and 8 months to be provided with an adoptive placement, compared with 12 months for the latter.

KEY FINDING

For the boys, white children had a significantly shorter duration of care prior to placement when compared with that of both the mixed parentage and black boys: 7 months as opposed to 10 and 12 months respectively.

* All Bonferroni tests performed at the 1 per cent level of significance.

† All differences between age groups within the two categories of gender were assessed using Bonferroni tests at the 1 per cent level of significance.

‡ This was the case in the inner London boroughs where minority ethnic children had waited 1 year 1 month for placement as opposed to 9 months for white children (F=4.286 df 1 at p<0.01). In metropolitan districts, comparable figures were 6 months for white children and 9 months for those of a minority ethnic background (F=10.387 df 1 at p<0.01). It was not possible to derive comparable figures for the other types of agency because of the small numbers of minority ethnic children.

The children's needs

Whilst the children's special needs were not found to have any clear impact on the overall duration of care prior to being approved for adoption by the agency, they tended to increase significantly the period of waiting for a suitable adoptive placement (see ANOVA summary Table in introduction).

This was true of both the child's developmental difficulties and health condition, but again it was essential to take into account the actual combination of needs with a variety of other factors. For example, needs arising from the child's heredity (see definition in Chapter 3) did not have any significant influence when considering the whole sample, but they were found to be relevant to the group of infants aged under 6 months at time of approval.

The impact of developmental problems

Let us begin with the influence of the child's developmental difficulties on the length of time between approval and placement with adopters. As indicated earlier, developmental and/or learning difficulties were found almost exclusively in the white children of the sample. The very few minority ethnic children with such difficulties were therefore excluded from the analysis.*

Concentrating therefore on the white children, the first important finding was that the effect of developmental difficulties was apparent for children between 6 to 30 months of age and, albeit less dramatic, for those in the under 6 months age band. By contrast, the impact of the child's developmental difficulties did not prove enduring in the older children aged 30 months and over.[†]

In the latter group, there was some evidence that other factors – including, of course, age itself – were more likely to account for delays experienced by the children while awaiting placement with adopters.

Within the 6–30 months age band, simple factorial analysis of variance pointed to a significant pattern of interaction between developmental difficulties, placement of sibling groups, gender and age. The white children in the sample were divided along these lines and outcomes for this procedure are summarised in Figure 5.7 below. Differences are examined amongst

Figure 5.7

The impact of the child's developmental difficulties on the time of waiting between "best interest" decision and placement with adopters: the interaction between developmental needs, age, placement of sibling groups and gender in the white children aged 6–30 months at approval

Note: Months. N=699 white children aged 6 to 30 months at time of assessment for adoption

No developmental need recorded

Developmental need

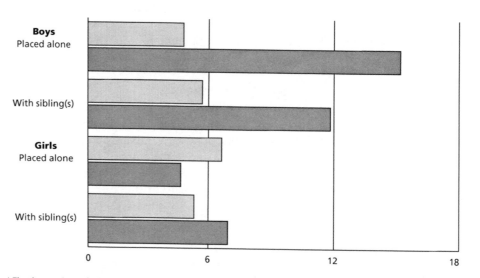

* The tiny numbers of mixed parentage and black children listed with developmental difficulties (N=9 and 3 respectively) did not permit any reliable assessment of significant differences in respect of the child's other characteristics.

† ANOVA statistics for time between "best interest" decision and placement by developmental needs across the 3 main categories of age were as follows: under 6 months (F=6.871 df 1 at p<0.01); 6–30 months (F=34.157 df 1 at p<0.01); 30 months and over (F=5.399 df 1 p=0.035 not significant at the 0.01 level).

categories of children in relation to time between approval and placement. For the purpose of the analysis, children placed individually are distinguished from those who were placed as part of a sibling group.

To summarise, the main conclusion to be drawn from the analysis was that the effect of developmental difficulties was greatly enhanced in the subset of boys aged 6–30 months when approved for adoption, differences being further accentuated in those who were placed for adoption individually. In the latter category, boys with developmental difficulties had waited on average 15 months to be placed with adopters as opposed to 5 months in those listed with no developmental and/or learning difficulties. The gap caused by developmental needs was reduced to 6 months in the white boys within the same age band placed as part of a sibling group.

In sharp contrast, none of the above differences were statistically significant when considering the adopted girls in the relevant group for comparison. For white girls aged 6–30 months at the time of approval, the presence of developmental difficulties did not increase the length of time waiting for placement, regardless of whether these girls were to be placed alone or with sibling(s).*

With regard to the younger white infants approved for adoption under the age of 6 months, developmental difficulties were found exclusively in the children placed individually and mostly among male infants; in this group, there were some differences according to the child's developmental difficulties. On average, the very young boys of the sample had been provided with placements within 2 months following approval for adoption. The comparable figure was 5 months in those who were described as having developmental difficulties.†

Consistent with previous considerations, no significant differences were found in any categories of children aged 30 months and over at the point of approval for adoption. When controlling for the interaction between gender and placement for siblings in that particular age band, there was no empirical evidence of any substantial gap induced by the presence of developmental needs in the children.‡

The child's medical condition

Did the child's medical condition have a similar effect on the children's duration of care between approval and placement? Preliminary analysis of variance pointed to the impact of health problems, with differences in periods of waiting between children with no medical record and those with a moderate medical condition, on the one hand, and children with severe health problems on the other.

The length of time spent prior to placement was influenced by the medical problems of the children when approved for adoption. Overall, the children with severe medical problems had waited an average of 13 months to be placed with adopters, as opposed to 8 months for the children with a moderate medical problem and 6 months for the rest of the sample.**

KEY FINDING

The impact of developmental difficulties was greatly enhanced in the subset of boys aged 6–30 months when approved for adoption, differences being further accentuated in those who were placed for adoption individually.

KEY FINDING

Differences were not statistically significant when considering the adopted girls in the relevant group for comparison.

KEY FINDING

The children with severe medical problems had waited an average of 13 months to be placed with adopters, as opposed to 8 months for the children with a moderate medical problem and 6 months for the rest of the sample.

---

* ANOVA statistics were as follows: boys placed alone (F=51.550 df 1 at p<0.01; % of explained variance=18.1; N=236); boys placed with sibling(s) (F=23.251 df 1 at p<0.01; % of explained variance=18.3; N=105); girls placed alone (F=1.598 df 1 at p=0.208 n.s.; N=218); girls placed with sibling(s) (F=1.626 df 1 at p=0.205 n.s.; N=110).

† F=7.170 df 1 at p<0.01; N=148 white boys approved for adoption under the age of 6 months and placed alone.

‡ ANOVA statistics for the "30 months+" age group were as follows: boys placed alone (F=4.515 df 1 at p=0.035 n.s.; N=150); boys placed with sibling(s) (F=4.206 df 1 at p=0.042 n.s.; N=178); girls placed alone (F=5.530 df 1 at p=0.061 n.s.; N=124); girls placed with sibling(s) (F=0.454 df 1 at p=0.674 n.s.; N=187).

** F=29.302 df 2 at p<0.01; Post hoc pairwise multiple comparisons with Bonferroni test at the 1 per cent level of significance.

These differences were assessed in the context of the child's gender and age at approval.*

In addition, the vast majority (91 per cent) of the children described as having serious health problems were white children. Taking account of the tiny numbers of mixed parentage (N=6) and black (N=2) children in the "serious medical condition" category, there was no way of assessing patterns of interaction between the child's ethnic origin and their health problems.

The main statistical effect of the child's medical condition on the length of time waiting for placement was consistent across both categories of gender in the children adopted during 1998/99 (see Table 5.2). Differences were particularly striking in the subset of boys: those with no medical condition had waited an average of 7 months as opposed to 14 months in those who were described as having serious health problems and, for some, life-limiting conditions.

Table 5.2

Time between "best interest" decision and placement: the impact of medical problems on the boys and girls in the sample

Note: N=1,783 children (information was missing in 18 cases). *Statistically significant at the 1 per cent level (Bonferroni test).

Health problems	Time between approval and placement Months	N	ANOVA Statistics			
			F	df	Sig.	per cent of varience
Boys						
None	7	(743)	19.545	2	p<0.01	4.1
Moderate	9	(110)				
Serious	14*	(53)				
Girls						
None	6	(772)	8.622	2	p<0.01	1.9
Moderate	6	(69)				
Serious	11*	(37)				

Moreover, the differences between children with severe health difficulties and all the other children of the same gender proved statistically significant for both boys and girls. The very specific profile of children described as having severe medical problems was confirmed in both groups of children classified according to gender.[†]

Looking at the age profile of the children showed that the above association between medical condition and the duration of care between approval and placement was only relevant to the subsets of children aged over 6 months at time of approval. The flow chart in Figure 5.8 displays differences graphically and provides a way to compare patterns of pre-placement time in care for the three main age groups when taking account of the child's health problems.

As can be seen, there was little variation in the infants aged under 6 months at approval and differences were not found statistically significant. In the rest of the adopted children, the impact of medical problems was increased by age.[‡]

Considering, for instance, the older children of the sample, the figure of a nine-month duration of care for children with no particular record of health problems compared with a total of 17 months in those described as having

---

* It should be remembered that medical problems were found to be over-represented amongst the boys. A total of 18 per cent were listed as children with either moderate or severe medical problems, as opposed to 13 per cent of the girls (see Chapter 3).

† Bonferroni test at the 1 per cent level of significance showed that children with a severe medical condition had significantly longer duration of care between approval and placement, whilst there were no differences amongst the other children (including those with moderate health problems).

‡ ANOVA statistics were as follows: under 6 months: F=2.722 df 2 at p=0.067 n.s.; 6–30 months: F=15.827 df 2 at p<0.01; % of explained variance = 4.1 per cent; 30 months and over: F=11.333 df 2 at p<0.01; % of explained variance = 3.2 per cent.

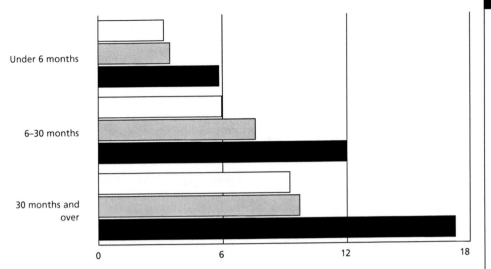

Figure 5.8

Time between "best interest" decision and placement: the impact of medical problems according to age of the child

Note: N=1,783 children (information was missing in 18 cases)

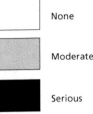

☐ None

▨ Moderate

■ Serious

severe difficulties. In the children aged 6 to 30 months at approval, the gap was slightly smaller with a difference of approximately 6 months between the two categories of children.

The findings for all the children aged 6 months and over provided further empirical evidence for previous comparison regarding differences between children with either a moderate medical condition or no specific health problems and those described as children with serious and/or life-limiting conditions.*

Needs arising from the child's heredity

A third important area of interest in relation to the child's special needs was that of the congenital risks and whether these may exert a significant influence on the process of placing children for adoption. Considering the whole cohort of children adopted during 1998/99, the analysis of factors of risk arising from the child's heredity failed to explain any variation in the total length of time in care prior to placement.

There was however some indication that these particular needs had weighted significantly on the period of waiting for placement in some groups of children. This was particularly true of the very young infants aged under 6 months at "best interest" decision, but did not apply to the older children in the sample (see Table 5.3).

KEY FINDING

Factors of risk arising from the child's heredity weighted significantly on the period of waiting for placement in some groups of children, particularly the very young infants aged under 6 months at "best interest" decision.

Table 5.3

Time between "best interest" decision and placement: the impact of genetic risks according to the child's age at approval for adoption

Note: N=1,783 children (information was missing in 18 cases).

Age at approval for adoption	Time between approval and placement Months	N	ANOVA Statistics		
			F	df	Sig.
Under 6 months					
No risk recorded	3	(286)	28.474	1	p<0.01
Risk arising from heredity	5	(65)			
6–30 months					
No risk recorded	6	(581)	0.791	1	p=0.374
Risk arising from heredity	6	(165)			
30 months and over					
No risk recorded	9	(600)	2.783	1	p=0.096
Risk arising from heredity	8	(86)			

• Post hoc pairwise multiple comparisons (Bonferroni test at p<0.01).

KEY FINDING

For the babies approved for adoption under 6 months, the increase produced by congenital risks in the length of time waiting for placement was of about 2 months. There was no evidence of a similar gap for the other children in the study.

For the infants approved for adoption under 6 months of age, the increase produced by congenital risks in the length of time waiting for placement was about 2 months, with an average of 5 months in the children listed with heredity factors as opposed to only 3 months in the rest of the very young infants. There was no evidence of a similar gap for the other children in the study (see ANOVA statistics in Table 5.3).

Legal status of child and birth mother's agreement

Returning to the first sequence of the adoption process, both the child's legal status and whether the birth mother had agreed to adoption were found to be influential factors of time in care prior to being identified for adoption (see previous section). Not surprisingly, the preceding part of the analysis showed that there was a strong relationship between the two variables (see Chapter 4).

Legal status at time of assessment

Similarly, the data concerning the duration of care between approval and placement showed that legal status had an impact for certain groups of children.

KEY FINDING

Children looked after under voluntary agreements were placed for adoption within a shorter period of time: approximately 5 months as opposed to 8 months in the children subject to care orders.

The general pattern was that children looked after under voluntary agreements were placed for adoption within a shorter period of time: approximately 5 months in the former as opposed to 8 months in the children subject to care orders (see ANOVA Table in the introduction). Comparable figures proved very consistent when controlling for the child's gender.*

KEY FINDING

The influence of legal proceedings was restricted to the white and mixed parentage children of the sample. For the black children, there was no significant variation in the time of waiting for placement according to the child's legal status.

In terms of the child's ethnic origin, the influence of legal proceedings was restricted to the white and mixed parentage children of the sample. For the black children adopted during 1998/99, there was no evidence of a significant variation in the time of waiting for placement according to the child's legal status: the average was 1 year both for black children looked after under voluntary agreements and for those in compulsory care.†

The most significant pattern of interaction was found when comparing legal status with the age profile of the children. As indicated earlier, there was a significant level of statistical association between the two variables, with older children being more likely to be the subjects of care orders.‡

KEY FINDING

Only infants aged under 6 months had distinct profiles: the average time of waiting for placement was 2 months for those looked after under section 20 compared with 4 months for those looked after under care orders.

Exploring differences induced by legal status in the context of the child's age at approval showed that only infants aged under 6 months had distinct profiles. In that particular age band, the average time of waiting for placement was 2 months for infants looked after under section 20 compared with 4 months for those who were looked after under care orders (see Table 5.4). Again, the findings highlighted the specificity of the infants relinquished for adoption by their birth parents: the overall rate of birth mother's agreement to adoption was as high as 99 per cent for the infants accommodated under voluntary agreements and approved under 6 months of age.

The child's legal status ceased to have influence in the other age bands, where the children were found to share fairly similar periods of waiting to join prospective adopters (see relevant ANOVA statistics in Table 5.4).

---

* Differences according to the child's legal status were statistically significant both in the boys and girls. Relevant ANOVA statistics were as follows: boys: $F=19.031$ df 1 at $p<0.01$; Girls: $F=22.799$ df 1 at $p<0.01$.

† Analysis of variance was conducted in the three groups of children according to ethnicity. White: $F=46.001$ df 1 at $p<0.01$; Mixed parentage: $F=6.596$ df 1 at $p<0.01$; Black: $F=0.007$ df 1 $p=0.934$ n.s. Caution must be exercised due to the small number of black children in the sample. "Black" is intended as African, African-Caribbean and Asian.

‡ Chi-Square statistics were as follows: legal status * age at "best interest" decision: $\chi^2=270.453$ df 2 $p<0.01$; Cramer's $V=0.389$.

Age at approval for adoption	Time between approval and placement Months	N	ANOVA Statistics		
			F	df	Sig.
Under 6 months					
Section 20	2	(189)	27.301	1	p<0.01
Care order	4	(161)			
6–30 months					
Section 20	5	(113)	3.393	1	p=0.06
Care order	7	(634)			
30 months and over					
Section 20	9	(84)	0.015	1	p=0.902
Care order	9	(602)			

Table 5.4

Time between "best interest" decision and placement: age and legal status at the time of approval for adoption

Note: N=1,783 children (information was missing in 18 cases).

KEY FINDING

The child's legal status ceased to have influence in the other age bands, where the children were found to share fairly similar periods of waiting to join prospective adopters.

KEY FINDING

Fifteen per cent of the infants in compulsory care were described as having health problems against only 5 per cent of those accommodated voluntarily.

KEY FINDING

Records of congenital risks were found in only 3 per cent of the infants looked after under section 20 as opposed to 37 per cent of those who were in compulsory care.

KEY FINDING

The impact of the birth mother's agreement to the decision to pursue adoption was restricted to young infants under the age of 6 months at the time of approval, with a significantly shorter duration of care in the children whose birth mothers had accepted the plan.

The understanding of the nature of the information contained in the two categories of legal status considered for the analysis is crucial. As discussed earlier, one can make the assumption that the type of legal proceedings that social services departments resort to in looking after the particular child is a crude indicator of the child's circumstances, history and special needs. Undoubtedly, it is those factors combined with the impact of legal proceedings which produce the most sizeable differences in the duration of care prior to placement with adopters.

Further examination of the "under 6 month" group of children helped reveal some important aspects of the children's profile in that particular age band. The first finding of interest was that of the statistical association between care orders and medical problems: 15 per cent of the infants in compulsory care were described as having health problems against only 5 per cent of those accommodated voluntarily.*

More significantly, perhaps, there was a strong relationship between care proceedings and the records of congenital risks: the latter needs were found in only 3 per cent of the infants looked after under section 20 as opposed to 37 per cent of those who were in compulsory care.†

Birth mother's agreement to the adoption plan

The exploration of the data concerning birth mothers' attitudes towards adoption showed very similar patterns.

Like legal status, the impact of the birth mother's agreement to the decision to pursue adoption was restricted to young infants under the age of 6 months at the time of approval, with a significantly shorter duration of care following the "best interest" decision in the children whose birth mothers had accepted the plan.

However, these differences reflected predominantly the influence of legal proceedings: adding the information about the birth mother's stance in respect of adoption did not produce any significant change in the overall pattern of variation according to the child's legal status.‡

* χ^2=12.674 df 2 at p<0.01; Cramer's V=0.190.

† χ^2=68.377 df 1 at p<0.01; Phi=0.441. In contrast, there was no evidence of any correlation between legal status and developmental problems in the "under 6 month" category of age: χ^2=1.084 df 1 p=0.298 n.s.

‡ The influence of the two main categories of legal proceedings was controlled for the agreement of birth mother. None of the relevant ANOVA statistics were found significant: Section 20* Birth mother agreement: F=2.429 df 1 p=0.120 n.s.; Care order*Birth mother agreement: F=1.643 df 1 p=0.200. (N=1,648 missing data in 153 children)

KEY FINDING

The extent of placement of sibling groups did not impact significantly on the length of time the children had waited prior to being provided with an adoptive placement.

Placement of sibling groups

Unlike most factors considered in the previous parts of the analysis, the extent of placement of sibling groups did not impact significantly on the length of time the children had waited prior to being provided with an adoptive placement. The variation that was identified by preliminary analysis of variance was mostly attributable to the age factor, which was closely inter-related with whether placement had been required for a single child or a group of siblings.*

As suggested at the beginning of this chapter, some of the factors that were relevant to the analysis of delays taking place prior to approval for adoption may not continue to be pertinent when considering the second main sequence of the process. Performing an analysis of variance specifying age at "best interest" decision as covariate revealed that differences were accounted for by the age profile rather than the number of children placed.†

Two points must be made here. First, it is important to stress the heterogeneity of the group of children placed individually. This category would indeed contain very young infants relinquished for adoption by their birth parents, but would also comprise children with special needs for whom it may take longer to find a suitable placement. Notably, in the older children of the sample, special needs arising from heredity, medical condition or developmental difficulties were found to be over-represented amongst children placed for adoption singly.‡

Second, it should be remembered that the analysis was mainly child-based and did not therefore take into account the complexity of placement of siblings, the balance of needs and the possible age gap within groups of children placed together. Clearly, there would be a need for further analysis of the survey material to establish the specific contribution of each of the above factors to the children's period of waiting for a suitable adoptive placement.

Foster carer adoption

KEY FINDING

Children adopted by their foster carers tended to wait longer for placement, with a mean duration of care of 8 months following approval as opposed to 7 months in the rest of the children. Differences were restricted to the subset of children placed alone.

Adoption of a child by foster carers was found to exert a significant impact on the length of time that elapsed between entry into care and the decision that the child should be considered for adoption. On average, children adopted by their foster carers had waited twice as long as the other children prior to being identified for adoption.

Performing a similar analysis for the second sequence of the adoption process revealed that children adopted by foster carers tended also to wait longer for placement, with a mean duration of care of 8 months following approval as opposed to 7 months in the rest of the children (see ANOVA table in the introduction).**

By "placement" we refer here to the actual date when the foster placement was turned into an adoptive placement following decision by the agency panel that adoption was in the child's best interest.

---

* Age at "best interest" decision * sibling group: χ^2=243.828 df 2 p<0.01; Cramer's V=0.370.

† Simple factorial ANOVA statistics were as follows: age at "best interest": F=69.796 df 1 at p<0.01; placement for sibling groups: F=1.292 df 1 p=0.256 n.s. Taking account of the actual size of the group of siblings to be placed showed no significant deviation from the above set of findings.

‡ In the "30 months and over" age band, children placed alone had more health and developmental problems (20 and 29 per cent respectively, as opposed to 11 and 20 % in those placed with siblings. Chi-Square statistics as follows: health: χ^2=19.312 df 2 at p<0.01; developmental difficulties: χ^2=7.156 df 1 at p<0.01). Single children aged 6 months and over at time of approval were presenting congenital risks in the proportion of 20 per cent compared with only 14 per cent in those placed as part of a sibling group (χ^2=7.037 df 1 at p<0.01).

** N=1,759 missing data in 42 children.

However, the overall effect was much less dramatic here, and was to a large extent dependent upon the age profile of the child.*

In Chapter 4 we found that children adopted by their foster carers tended to be older. More specifically, however, there was some evidence of a more complex pattern of interaction between age, gender, foster carer adoption and the number of children placed.

First, differences were restricted to the subset of children placed alone. In cases where placement had been achieved for a group of at least two siblings, there was no indication of any increase in the duration of care prior to placement for the children adopted by their foster carers. On the contrary, differences held true in the group of children placed individually, and the pattern was consistent across all categories of age at approval.†

Second, there was substantial variation in the impact of adoption by foster carers when taking account of the age of child at "best interest" decision. As illustrated in Figure 5.9, children adopted by their foster carers tended to wait longer for placement in both the "under 6 months" and "6–30 months" age bands. Differences were not statistically significant within the "30 months–5 years" age group. In contrast, the pattern found in the older children aged 5 years and over at time of approval was one of the children adopted by foster carers waiting significantly shorter time for placement (6 months) when compared with those placed with a "new" adoptive family (12 months).‡

5 Timing of procedures

KEY FINDING

Children adopted by their foster carers tended to wait longer for placement in both the "under 6 months" and "6–30 months" age bands. In contrast, the pattern found in the older children aged 5 years+ was one of the children adopted by foster carers waiting significantly shorter time for placement.

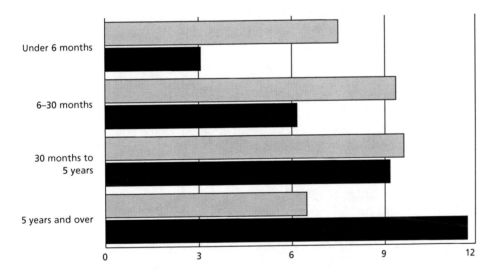

Under 6 months

6–30 months

30 months to 5 years

5 years and over

0   3   6   9   12

Figure 5.9

Time between "best interest" decision and placement: age at approval and adoption by foster carer(s)

Note: Months. N=1,783 children (information was missing in 43 children in the sample). Age at "best interest" decision was broken down into 4 main categories for the purpose of the analysis.

Foster carer(s)

New family

All differences were further accentuated when considering exclusively the children placed for adoption individually. This was particularly salient among older children aged 5 years and over at time of approval: single children adopted by their foster carers had waited less than 2 months before the foster placement was turned into an adoptive one. This compared with an average of 14 months in the single children placed with families unknown to them.**

Concentrating still on that particular subset of children aged 5 years and

* Simple factorial ANOVA: age at "best interest" decision: F=3.460 df 4 at p<0.01; Foster carer adoption: F=4.827 df 3 p=0.028 n.s. Two-way interaction: F=11.394 df 4 at p<0.01. N=1,759 missing data in 42 children.

† Single child: F=13.174 df 1 at p<0.01; Children placed with sibling(s): F=0.341 df 1 p=0.560 n.s.

‡ For the purpose of the analysis, it was important to isolate the older children aged 5 years+ at time of approval for adoption, as there was a great deal of evidence that these children had a distinct profile in relation to foster carer adoption. ANOVA statistics were as follows: Under 6 months: F=22.798 df 1 at p<0.01; 6–30 months: F=12.025 df 1 at p<0.01; 30 months-5 years: F=0.148 df 1 p=0.701 n.s.; 5 years and over: F=12.410 df 1 at p<0.01.

** N=All 247 children aged 5 years+ at approval. ANOVA: F=36.099 df 1 at p<0.01; total of explained variance = 26.3 per cent.

over and placed singly, the gender profile of the child was found to increase the existing gap between foster carer adoptions and the other cases. Differences were significantly larger in the boys: they had waited an average of 1 month for placement when adopted by foster carers. The comparable figure for the single boys aged 5 years and over, and placed with "new" adopters was 16 months. In the girls, the comparable figures were 2 and 11 months respectively.*

Although statistically significant, all the above considerations must be qualified by the specificity of adoption by foster carers. In many respects, the significance of the actual period of waiting for the foster placement to be turned into an adoptive one could not be addressed from the survey material. For instance, it was not possible to determine whether there had been any attempt to find a new adoptive placement for the particular child before adoption by foster carers. Similarly, delays relating to the process of approving foster carers as prospective adopters cannot be excluded.

5.2.3 Achieving adoption for looked after children

In this last section, the focus is on the third phase of the adoption process, that is, the sequence between the point of placement with adopters and the adoption order being granted by the court. As pointed out in the introduction, problems of post-placement delays have been frequently identified among other research samples and variation in these have often been found to be associated with features of the agency adoption policy and practice.

In particular, previous research has pointed to the significance of the extent to which local authorities may decide to apply for the granting of freeing orders by the courts.[†]

Unfortunately, information about freeing was not available from the survey data. It was therefore not possible to assess the impact of other important factors in the context of legal proceedings, and to establish whether the use of freeing orders by social services departments was likely to shorten the period of time waiting for the making of the adoption order.

Nor was there any indication of the reasons why children may have waited following placement with adopters. Clearly, there are a variety of reasons that may account for delays in achieving adoption, such as lengthy court proceedings, the need for assessment of both the stability and the suitability of placement by the authority, the importance of the child's views being sought, or agencies facing disagreement with the adoption plan on the part of the child's birth parents.

Bearing these limitations in mind, the study revealed that only some of the factors which weighted on the process of placing looked after children were also likely to have a significant influence on how the adoption was finalised (see relevant statistics in Table 5.5).

In addition, the analysis found that some factors, which had not proved operative in the preceding phases of the process, were likely to exert a significant influence on the time of waiting for adoption. This was the case, for example, with regard to the child's experience of sexual abuse, and also

---

* ANOVA statistics as follows: Boys: $F=20.031$ df 1 at $p<0.01$ (explained variance = 27.8 per cent); Girls: $F=16.291$ df 1 at $p<0.01$ (explained variance = 26.2 per cent).

† The impact of freeing was for instance discernible in all categories of children adopted from care during 1996. Children freed for adoption were found to have a shorter overall duration of care when compared with non freed children in the relevant group, mainly because freeing shortened the duration of adoptive placement prior to the order, but was consistently associated with a longer period of waiting for placement. One exception to this was found in infants relinquished by birth parents (see Ivaldi, 1998).

Child's characteristics	From placement to adoption	ANOVA statistics		
	Deviation from sample mean	df	F	% of variance
Ethnicity (3 groups)		2	4.871	0.5
Mixed parentage	+ 6 weeks			
Black*	+ 4 months			
Legal status (2 groups)		1	39.900	2.2
Section 20	– 3 months			
Sexual abuse		2	29.346	3.2
Possible	+ 5 weeks			
Definite	+ 12 months			
Placement for sib-group		1	51.205	2.8
Child with sibling(s)	+ 10 weeks			
Birth mother's disagreement	+ 2 weeks	1	5.930	0.4
Type of authority		4	36.833	7.7
Shire county	–			
Metropolitan district	– 4 weeks			
Unitary authority	– 3 months			
Inner London borough	+ 8 months			
Outer London borough	+ 5 months			
Age at placement with adopters		4	70.437	13.7
Under 6 months	– 6 months			
6–12 months	– 3 months			
12–30 months	– 2 months			
30 months–5 years	+ 7 weeks			
5 years and over	+ 6 months			

Table 5.5

Factors impacting on the period of time from placement to adoption: main statistical effects and deviation from mean in the whole sample

Note: ANOVA statistics. All values of the F statistic significant at $p<0.01$. N=1,783 (information missing in 18 children). * "Black" refers to African, African-Caribbean and Asian.

the type of local authority looking after the particular child, whilst other factors such as gender or the child's special needs arising from heredity and developmental difficulties were not found to be statistically associated with the length of time between placement and adoption.*

In the following sections, we examine the above patterns of association in the light of existing interactions between some of the most influential variables, and look for significant differences accounted for by the combination of factors.

Age at placement with adopters

Comparing patterns of interaction between age and periods of waiting in each of the preceding phases of the adoption process, there was some evidence of a linear increase in the length of time between placement and adoption across the age spectrum. The older the children at placement, the longer they were likely to wait for the adoption order to be granted by the court (see Figure 5.10).†

At one end of the age scale, babies placed under the age of 6 months had waited an average of 8 months before adoption, which compared with a mean duration as long as 1 year 8 months for the older children aged 5 and over when joining adopters (see relevant ANOVA statistics in the introduction to this section).

KEY FINDING

There was a linear increase in the length of time between placement and adoption across the age spectrum. The impact of age on the time of waiting for adoption proved remarkably consistent in all categories of children in the sample.

* ANOVA tests did not meet the $p<0.01$ criterion of statistical significance when applied to the following variables: gender: F=0.004 df 1 p=0.952 n.s.; developmental difficulties: F=0.941 df 1 p=0.332 n.s.; health problems: F=1.132 df 2 p=0.323 n.s.; congenital risks: F=1.085 df 1 p=0.298 n.s.; physical abuse: F=0.006 df 1 p=0.937 n.s.; foster carer adoption: F=3.872 df 1 p=0.049 n.s.

† NOTE: Pearson's r=0.325 significant at $p<0.01$, 2-tailed; both variables expressed in number of days; N=1,783.

Figure 5.10

Time between placement and adoption by age of the child at placement

Note: Months. N=1,783 children (information was missing in 18 cases)

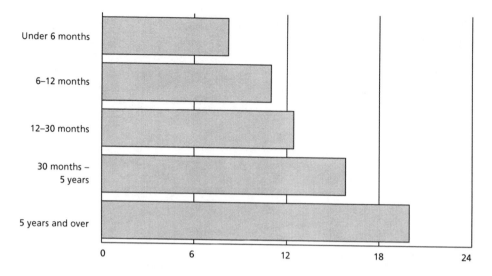

However, it should be noted that the differences between children aged 6–12 months and those aged 12–30 months were not found to be statistically significant.*

Controlling for other important characteristics of the children showed no significant variation in this general pattern of statistical association. The impact of age on the time of waiting for adoption proved remarkably consistent in all categories of children in the sample.†

Of particular interest, perhaps, was that the significance of age at placement was confirmed across all types of agency in the study. While there was some variation in how particular types of local authority seemed to have progressed through the post-placement phase, the age profile of the child remained a determinant factor of the length of time needed to finalise adoption.

Ethnic origin of the child

As indicated in the previous part of this section, the child's ethnicity was found to exert a significant effect on the process of placing children for adoption. The analysis also revealed an interesting combination of ethnic background, gender and age at approval for adoption. Was ethnicity still an important factor in the length of time waiting for adoption to be finalised and was it possible to draw a similar conclusion with regard to how the ethnic origin may combine with other crucial aspects of the children's profile?

First, it must be stressed that the overall effect of the child's ethnic background was significantly less dramatic when considering the last stage of the adoption process, and was by no means comparable, for example, to the gap that was found between the various categories of age.‡

Only the black children of the sample had a significantly longer duration of care after placement, with an average of 1 year 6 months against 1 year 3 months and 1 year 2 months for the mixed parentage and white children respectively.**

* All differences statistically significant at the 0.01 level (post hoc pairwise multiple comparisons with Bonferroni test) with the exception of the comparison between the children aged 6–12 months with those falling into the 12–30 months group of age (mean difference=44 days; p=0.398 n.s.).

† A series of simple factorial analyses of variance were conducted for age at placement together with each of the following factors: gender, ethnicity (3 groups), legal status (2 groups), type of agency (5 categories), placement of sibling group and birth mother's agreement to adoption. All F statistics for the main effect of age at placement were significant at p<0.01.

‡ Ethnicity alone had very little explanatory power with less than 0.5 per cent of explained variance, as opposed to 13.7 per cent for age at placement.

** Performing post-hoc comparison showed that differences between the white and mixed parentage children were not statistically significant (p=0.301 n.s.). "Black" refers to African, African-Caribbean and Asian.

This moderate impact of ethnicity was apparent across all groups of age at placement with adopters.*

Interestingly, differences were restricted to the girls of the sample and did not prove statistically significant for the boys. In the former category, black girls had waited on average 1 year 6 months for the adoption order to be granted, as opposed to 14 months and 16 months in the white and mixed parentage girls respectively.†

A similar conclusion was drawn from exploring the interaction between ethnicity and legal status: in all the children looked after under care orders, the analysis found no significant differences across children classified according to ethnicity. In contrast, there was a substantial increase in the length of time waiting for adoption for black children accommodated under voluntary agreements (1 year 5 months) when compared with the mixed parentage (14 months) and white children (11 months) in the relevant group of legal status.‡

This pattern of difference between black children, on the one hand, and the mixed parentage and white children on the other, was not reproduced when controlling for the number of children placed for adoption. There was no significant relationship between ethnicity and delays in finalising adoption for the children placed individually.**

For those placed with siblings, differences were mostly between the white and mixed parentage children: the former had waited an average of 1 year and 4 months for adoption, against 1 year and 11 months in the children with a dual heritage.††

More importantly, however, the effect of ethnicity was largely cancelled by considering the main type of local authority where the children originated.‡‡

As we shall see, there are important aspects of local authorities' attitudes towards adoption which may help to account for delays encountered by some of the children adopted from care during 1998/99. It is very likely that the variation observed between agencies in respect of the length of time needed to finalise adoption can be seen as reflecting differences in agency practice rather than the sole impact of the children's personal characteristics and needs.

Children sexually abused

Unlike the initial stages of the adoption process, the children's experience of sexual abuse – or the likelihood of it – had a significant influence on the overall duration of placement prior to adoption (see introduction to this section). In these children, there was clearly a strong likelihood of the relevant local authority allocating more time to assess the viability of the adoptive placement before proceeding with adoption or, alternatively, for the adopters wishing to ensure the placement was stable.

* Simple factorial ANOVA specifying "age at placement" as a quantitative covariate: $F=7.409$ df 2 at $p<0.01$.

† ANOVA statistics: Boys: $F=0.735$ df 2 $p=0.480$ n.s.; Girls: $F=5.654$ df 2 at $p<0.01$. In the girls of the sample, the only significant differences were between the black and white children (Bonferroni tests at $p<0.01$). "Black" refers to African, African-Caribbean and Asian.

‡ Care order: $F=2.393$ df 2 $p=0.092$ n.s.; Section 20: $F=8.170$ df 2 at $p<0.01$.

** Children placed alone: $F=3.059$ df 2 $p=0.047$ n.s. (N=1,143).

†† $F=10.896$ df 2 $p<0.01$ (N=658 children placed as part of a sibling group). Pairwise comparison using Bonferroni tests at $p<0.01$. The sample of black children placed with siblings was too small in size to allow a reliable assessment of the differences.

‡‡ Simple factorial ANOVA: type of authority: $F=12.909$ df 4 $p<0.01$; ethnicity: $F=1.579$ df 2 $p=0.206$ n.s. F-Statistics for each of the 5 main categories of agency were as follows: Shire County: $F=0.347$ df 2 $p=0.707$ n.s.; Metropolitan District: $F=0.958$ df 2 $p=0.384$ n.s.; Unitary Authority: $F=12.933$ df 2 at $p<0.01$; caution must be exercised here because of the small number of black children (N=7); Inner London Borough: $F=1.239$ df 2 $p=0.294$ n.s.; Outer London Borough: $F=0.705$ df 2 $p=0.796$ n.s.

As can be seen from Figure 5.11, children described as having suffered sexual abuse had a considerably longer time in placement prior to adoption, with an average of 2 years 2 months. In contrast, children for whom there was the indication of "possible" sexual abuse had waited 1 year 3 months, that is a very similar duration of placement to that of the children with no particular record (1 year 2 months).*

Figure 5.11

Time between placement and adoption in the children described as "sexually abused"

Note: Months. N=1,783 children (information was missing in 18 cases).

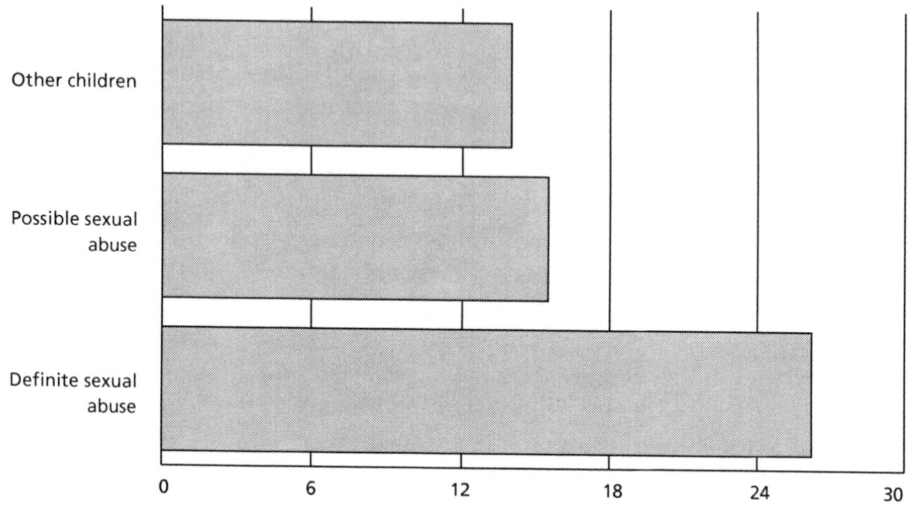

The above differences proved statistically robust across all age groups, although there was no indication of any particular interaction between age and sexual abuse.[†]

KEY FINDING

Experiences of sexual abuse had no clear impact on the time of waiting for placement in the subset of girls, whilst differences were further accentuated in the boys.

Nor was there any variation according to the child's legal status. As explained earlier in this study, all the children who were described as having suffered potential or definite sexual abuse were looked after under compulsory care proceedings (see Chapter 3). When compared with the other children in this legal category, the sexually abused children had persistently longer duration of placement prior to adoption.[‡]

In contrast, there was some variation when taking account of the gender of the child. Experiences of sexual abuse had no clear impact on the time of waiting for placement in the subset of girls, while differences were further accentuated in the boys.**

In the latter group, the length of time waiting for the adoption order was found to increase with the likelihood of the child having suffered from sexual abuse (see Figure 5.12).

The mean duration of placement was 1 year 1 month in the boys with no specific record of abuse. The comparable figure was already substantially higher in those who had been potentially the victims of sexual abuse, with an average of 1 year 7 months, and higher for the boys for whom "definite sexual" abuse had been referred to by the relevant case worker when preparing the child for adoption (2 years 7 months).[††]

* Differences were not statistically significant when comparing children with a record of 'possible sexual abuse' with those who had no particular record (post hoc pairwise multiple comparisons with Bonferroni test at the 0.01 level).

† Simple factorial ANOVA: Age at placement (covariate): F=196.941 df 1 at p<0.01; Sexual abuse: F=15.665 df 2 at p<0.01.

‡ F=24.215 df 2 at p<0.01 (N=1,413 children under care orders). Again, differences were exclusively between cases where there was a record of 'definite sexual' abuse on the one hand, and the rest of the children in the sample on the other hand (Bonferroni tests at p<0.01).

** ANOVA statistics: Girls: F=2.767 df 2 p=0.063 n.s.; Boys: F=32.041 df 2 at p<0.01.

†† All pairwise comparisons significant at the 0.01 level (Bonferroni test).

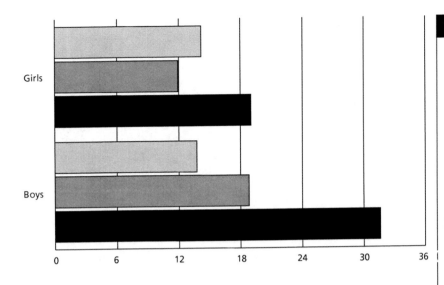

Figure 5.12

Time between placement and adoption in the children "sexually abused": a comparison between boys and girls

Note: Months. N=1,783 children (information was missing in 18 cases).

- Other children
- Possible sexual abuse
- Definite sexual abuse

Sibling groups

Children who had been placed with one or more birth siblings had significantly longer duration of placement prior to adoption. In the whole 1998/99 cohort, the gap between children placed individually and those placed as part of a sibling group was of approximately 3-and-a-half months (see relevant statistics in introduction).

As shown in Table 5.6, the impact of the actual number of children placed for adoption was not comparable across age bands. Differences between single children and sibling groups were only relevant to the 12–30 months age band: in the latter age group, children placed with birth siblings had waited for 1 year 2 months as opposed to 11 months for those placed individually. In the rest of the adopted children, there were no significant differences according to whether the children had been placed singly or with siblings.

The increase in the period of waiting for adoption for children placed with siblings was found in all types of local authority: controlling for the main categories of agency showed no significant deviation from the above pattern

KEY FINDING

Differences between single children and sibling groups were only relevant to the 12–30 months age band: in that age group, children placed with birth siblings had waited for 1 year 2 months as opposed to 11 months for those placed individually.

Table 5.6

Duration of adoptive placement prior to the making of the adoption order: age at placement and number of children placed

Note: N=1,783 children (information was missing in 18 cases)

Age at placement	Time between placement and adoption (years:months)	N	ANOVA Statistics F	df	Sig.
Under 6 months					
Single child	0:8	(183)	0.469	1	p=0.494
Placed with sibling(s)	0:7	(10)			
6–12 months					
Single child	0:10	(218)	6.129	1	p=0.014
Placed with sibling(s)	1:1	(41)			
12–30 months					
Single child	0:11	(354)	16.338	1	p<0.01
Placed with sibling(s)	1:2	(142)			
30 months–5 years					
Single child	1:4	(213)	0.423	1	p=0.516
Placed with sibling(s)	1:3	(246)			
5 years and over					
Single child	1:8	(165)	0.084	1	p=0.772
Placed with sibling(s)	1:7	(212)			

and confirmed the likelihood that children placed as part of a sibling group would wait longer.*

Variation in agency practice?

One last area of interest was that of the social services departments' responses in meeting the needs of children placed by them for adoption. When referring to possible causes of delay in achieving adoption for looked after children, figures for time in placement prior to adoption concealed significant variation between the main types of local authority (see introduction).

Notably, a great variation was found in duration of adoptive placements according to the type of agency. There was a clear tendency for children adopted from London boroughs to have longer placement periods prior to being adopted (see Figure 5.13). This was particularly true of the children placed by the inner London boroughs, who had on average waited 1 year 10 months for the making of the adoption order.

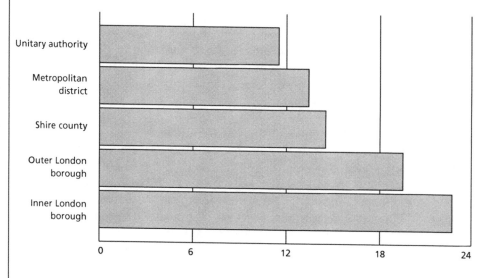

KEY FINDING

There was a clear tendency for children adopted from London Boroughs to have longer placement periods prior to being adopted.

Figure 5.13

Time between placement and adoption: variation between the main types of local authority (DoH classification)

Note: Months. N=1,783 children (information was missing in 18 cases).

The comparable figure in the outer areas of London was 1 year 7 months. In contrast, children adopted from shire counties and metropolitan districts had a mean duration of placement of 14 and 13 months respectively. The shortest placement time prior to adoption was found in the children adopted from unitary authorities, with an average of 11 months.

The above statistical association between type of agency and the length of time spent in placement prior to adoption held true when controlled for the age profile of the children. Regardless of the child's age at placement, it was still possible to distinguish between children adopted from the London areas and the rest of the children in the sample.[†]

KEY FINDING

Discrepancies observed between agencies in terms of duration of adoptive placements might be partly due to variation in the use of freeing orders.

Neither gender nor legal status of child made any significant alteration to that particular model, bearing in mind, however, that the legal status referred to in this part of the analysis reflects the child's situation at time of approval for adoption and would therefore not include any subsequent change in legal procedures such as the granting of freeing orders or shifts from voluntary agreements to compulsory care proceedings.[‡]

* Simple factorial analysis of variance: Type of agency: $F=43.929$ df 4 at $p<0.01$; Placement for sibling groups: $F=54.565$ df 1 at $p<0.01$.

† Simple factorial analysis of variance specifying age as a covariate: age at placement: $F=230.955$ df 1 at $p<0.01$; type of local authority: $F=42.162$ df 4 at $p<0.01$.

‡ Two simple factorial analyses of variance were performed. 1/ Type of local authority: $F=39.793$ df 4 at $p<0.01$; gender: $F=0.050$ df 1 $p=0.824$ n.s. 2/ Type of local authority: $F=30.088$ df 4 at $p<0.01$; legal status: $F=32.690$ df 1 at $p<0.01$.

The child's ethnic origin also applied to differences across categories of agency. London children waited longer for adoption following placement across all categories of ethnicity in the study.*

The above results broadly confirmed those of the previous study (Ivaldi, 1998) of the cohort of children who had left care for adoption during 1996, which pointed to greater delay in finalising adoption for the group of children adopted from London local authorities. The main assumption on which that analysis rested was that the discrepancies observed between agencies in terms of duration of adoptive placements might be partly due to variation in the use of legal procedures available to child care workers and agency adoption panels (Dance, 1997; Murch and Lowe, 1993).

Related to that hypothesis was the impact of freeing on the overall duration of placement: the data showed that freeing orders tended to shorten substantially the length of time in placement prior to adoption. Concurrently, the "London" figures revealed a relatively low use of freeing for adoption provisions by comparison with shire counties and metropolitan boroughs.[†]

As acknowledged in our previous study (Ivaldi, 1998), it would be useful to examine whether the practice of the London courts was influential in determining the extent to which freeing orders were sought by particular agencies.

Turning back to the 1998/99 cohort of children adopted from care, the lack of survey data concerning the use of freeing did not allow further investigation of the extent to which individual agencies had resorted to freeing provisions in achieving adoption for their children. It was, however, possible to complement the above analysis with details of the birth mother's agreement to the adoption plan by the relevant authority.

Type of local authority	Time between placement and adoption Yrs:mths	N	ANOVA Statistics		
			F	df	Sig.
Shire county					
Birth mother disagreed	1:2	(285)	0.070	1	p=0.792
Birth mother agreed	1:2	(284)			
Metropolitan district					
Birth mother disagreed	1:1	(359)	1.988	1	p=0.159
Birth mother agreed	1:0	(187)			
Unitary authority					
Birth mother disagreed	1:0	(207)	0.712	1	p=0.399
Birth mother agreed	0:11	(162)			
Inner London borough					
Birth mother disagreed	2:1	(55)	6.928	1	p<0.01
Birth mother agreed	1:5	(32)			
Outer London borough					
Birth mother disagreed	1:10	(48)	8.010	1	p<0.01
Birth mother agreed	1:5	(59)			

Table 5.7

Duration of adoptive placement prior to the making of the adoption order: type of local authority and birth mother's agreement to adoption

Note: N=1,648 children (information was missing in 153 cases)

* Simple factorial analysis of variance: type of local authority: F=12.909 df 4 at p<0.01; ethnicity: F=1.579 df 1 p=0.206 n.s. The results relevant to the black children should however be interpreted with some caution as the total number of Asian, African and African-Caribbean children in the sample was small.

† The wide variation in the use of freeing for adoption provisions across types of local authority was consistently evidenced by comparable figures derived for 1994 and 1995. Over a three-year period of time, both shire county and metropolitan district social services emerged as higher users of freeing while local authorities in London areas did not seem to use freeing quite as much as agencies in other parts of the country (see Ivaldi, 1998).

While the latter factor was not found to impact significantly on the duration of placement in the sample as a whole, it was interesting to note that there were substantial differences in both the inner and outer areas of London. Table 5.7 contains information about birth mothers' attitudes towards adoption as derived from the broad categorisation of agency in the study, together with relevant statistics regarding time in placement.

As can be seen from Table 5.7, the issue of birth mother's consent was only relevant to the inner and outer London boroughs, where disagreement was found to increase the overall duration of placement prior to the making of the adoption order by the Court, with gaps of 8 and 5 months respectively. Comparable figures for shire counties, metropolitan districts and unitary authorities showed no significant differences according to whether birth mothers had agreed to the adoption plan.

One possible assumption behind these results is that the lower use of freeing orders by London social services deparments may allow the issue of birth mother's agreement to have a significant impact on the time needed to finalise adoption, while in other types of local authority the use of freeing may help circumvent the delays that can arise in contested adoptions.

References

Dance, C (1997) *Focus on Adoption – A snapshot of adoption patterns in England – 1995*, London: BAAF.

Ivaldi, G (1998) *Children Adopted from Care: An examination of agency adoptions in England – 1996*, London: BAAF.

Murch, M Lowe, N Borkowski, M Copner, R and Griew, K (1993) *Pathways to Adoption*, University of Bristol, Socio-Legal Centre for Family Studies, London: HMSO.

The birth families

Another important aim of the adoption survey was to gather information about birth parents. It is true to say that the social and demographics factors of care have been well documented by previous research, but there has been relatively little attention given to the profile and characteristics of birth families whose children are adopted from local authority care every year.

Although not the main focus of the study, the process of collecting data on the children adopted out of care during 1998/99 via existing assessment forms allowed simultaneous investigation of some important aspects of the 1,448 birth families involved.

The findings in this chapter are organised around three main features. In the first section we look at the profile of the birth parents in the study sample, particularly in terms of their age at birth of child, ethnicity and religious affiliation. In the second section we examine the birth parent's marital status at the time of "best interest" decision (i.e. that the child should be adopted) together with some occupational data. The third and last section concentrates on the issue of parental responsibility.

6.1 The profile of birth parents

This first section explores the characteristics of the 1,448 birth families by looking at their age profile, ethnicity and religious denomination. It must be stressed here that there were limitations on the data collected from participating local authorities. In particular, some important details of the birth fathers' social and demographic characteristics were not systematically recorded on the assessment Form E. It was not possible to establish from the forms why the information had not been recorded.

6.1.1 Age at birth of child

The mean age of birth mothers at time of child's birth was 24 years 11 months. Birth fathers were found to be slightly older with an average of 29 years 5 months. The youngest birth mother was 13 years 10 months, and the youngest father was 14 years.*

Twelve per cent of the birth mothers were under the age of 18, as opposed to 4 per cent of the fathers. The peak age band in both groups was 25–34 years with 40 and 47 per cent of the mothers and fathers respectively in that age category. Another 39 per cent of the mothers were aged 18–24 years compared with 27 per cent of the fathers. "Older" birth parents aged 35 years and over at birth of child were in the minority and represented 22 per cent of the fathers and only 9 per cent of the mothers (see Figure 6.1).

6.1.2 Ethnicity

Consistent with preceding findings concerning adopted children, the vast majority of birth parents were white: 94 and 92 per cent of the mothers and fathers respectively. It was interesting to note, however, that, by comparison with the children, cases of mixed parentage parents were under-represented in the minority ethnic birth parents. Of the 87 mothers of a minority ethnic background, only 40 per cent were of mixed parentage (as opposed to nearly

> **KEY FINDING**
>
> The mean age of birth mothers at time of child's birth was 24 years and 11 months. Birth fathers were found to be slightly older with an average of 29 years and 5 months.

> **KEY FINDING**
>
> Young birth mothers under the age of 18 years accounted for 12 per cent of the family sample.

> **KEY FINDING**
>
> The vast majority of birth parents were white: 94 and 92 per cent of the mothers and fathers respectively.

* N=1,353 birth mothers and 997 birth fathers. Information was missing in 95 and 451 birth mothers and fathers respectively.

Figure 6.1

Age of birth parents at time of child's birth

Note: Expressed as a percentage of all birth mothers and all birth fathers. N=1,353 birth mothers (missing information in 95 cases), N=997 birth fathers (no date of birth was recorded for 451 fathers in the sample)

Percentage of birth mothers

Percentage of birth fathers

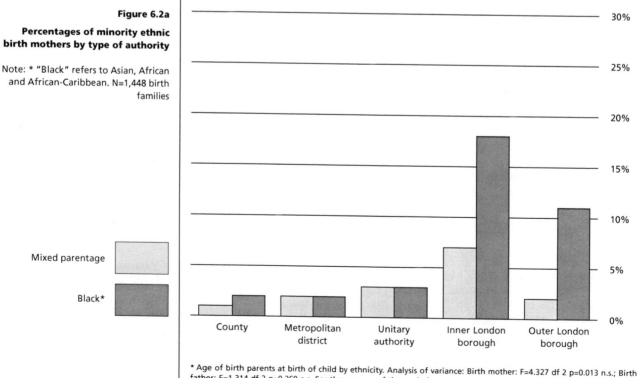

KEY FINDING

Cases of mixed parentage parents were under-represented in the minority ethnic birth parents.

three-quarters of the children, see Chapter 3). Another 37 per cent were African and African-Caribbean, and 23 per cent were Asian.

Of the minority ethnic birth fathers, only 21 per cent were of mixed parentage. Half (50 per cent) were African and African-Caribbean, and nearly a third (29 per cent) were of Asian ethnic background.

Looking at the age of parents at child's birth by ethnicity showed no statistically significant differences and the age profile of birth parents of a minority ethnic background was very similar to that of the white parents in the sample.*

There was substantial variation in the proportion of African, African-Caribbean and Asian birth parents across the main types of local authority

Figure 6.2a

Percentages of minority ethnic birth mothers by type of authority

Note: * "Black" refers to Asian, African and African-Caribbean. N=1,448 birth families

Mixed parentage

Black*

* Age of birth parents at birth of child by ethnicity. Analysis of variance: Birth mother: F=4.327 df 2 p=0.013 n.s.; Birth father: F=1.314 df 2 p=0.269 n.s. For the purpose of the analysis, parents were grouped into 3 ethnic categories: white, mixed parentage and black. "Black" refers here to African, African-Caribbean and Asian.

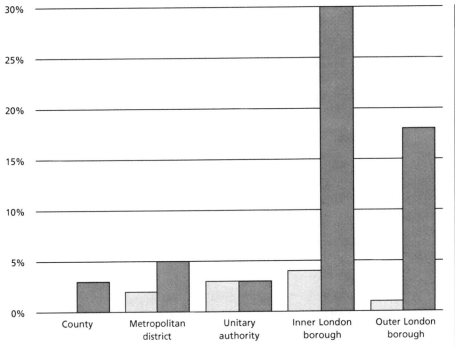

Figure 6.2b

Percentages of minority ethnic birth fathers by type of authority
Note: * "Black" refers to Asian, African and African-Caribbean. N=1,448 birth families

Mixed parentage

Black*

which was consistent with previous findings concerning the children adopted during 1998/99. However, it was clear that black parents were over-represented in the London area (see Figures 6.2a & b).

A total of 18 and 11 per cent respectively of the birth mothers in the inner and outer London boroughs were black as opposed to about 3 per cent in the other categories of local authority. Similarly, black fathers were found in a greater proportion in the inner areas of London (30 per cent) and, to a lesser extent, in the outer London boroughs (18 per cent). These figures compared with percentages varying between 3 and 5 per cent in the remaining types of agency.*

6.1.3 Religious affiliation

Like the children, information about birth parents' religious affiliation had not been systematically recorded on the assessment forms. This was particularly true of the birth fathers with the relevant information missing in nearly half (49 per cent) of the cases (see Table 6.1). Indications of religious denomination or the lack of it were recorded for 79 per cent of the birth mothers.

Table 6.1

Religious denomination of birth parents
Note: As recorded on assessment material at time of approval of child for adoption (N=1,448 birth families). * "Other Protestant": not Church of England. ** "Other religion" includes: Jehovah's Witness, Jewish, Mormon, Hindu, Buddhist, and Greek Orthodox.

	N	Birth mother		N	Birth father	
		per cent of all cases	per cent of cases where religious denomination was recorded		per cent of all cases	per cent of cases where religious denomination was recorded
None	291	20	25	219	15	30
Church of England	544	38	47	343	24	47
Catholic	178	12	15	94	6	13
Other Protestant*	94	6	8	51	3	7
Muslim	16	1	2	10	1	1
Other religion**	28	2	3	18	1	2
Total	1,151	79	100	735	51	100
Not specified on form	297	21		713	49	
TOTAL	1,448	100		1,448	100	

* These differences were statistically significant: birth mother: χ^2=87.824 df 8 at p<0.01; Cramer's V=0.174; Birth father: χ^2=138.559 df 8 at p<0.01; Cramer's V=0.219. 'Black' refers here to African, African-Caribbean and Asian.

Of the 1,150 cases where the religious denomination of the birth mother was recorded, nearly half (47 per cent) were Church of England. Another 15 per cent were Catholic while a quarter (25 per cent) had no specific religion and 8 per cent were recorded as being from another Protestant background. Percentages were very similar in the 735 birth fathers for whom religious data were available (see Table 6.1).

6.2 Marital status and occupation

In this second section we turn to the analysis of the birth parents' marital status and occupation at the time of assessment of child for adoption. Again, there were some limitations on the availability of data and figures could only be derived for a sub-sample of birth mothers and fathers for whom records were comprehensive.

6.2.1 Marital status

The majority of birth parents were single at the time of "best interest" decision; nearly two-thirds (65 per cent) of the birth mothers and 59 per cent of the birth fathers for whom information had been recorded (see Figure 6.3).

Figure 6.3

Marital status of birth parents at time of "best interest" decision

Note: N=1,419 birth mothers (missing cases = 29); N=1,093 birth fathers (missing = 355).
* "Other" refers to widow/widower or birth parent deceased.

Percentage of all birth mothers

Percentage of all birth fathers

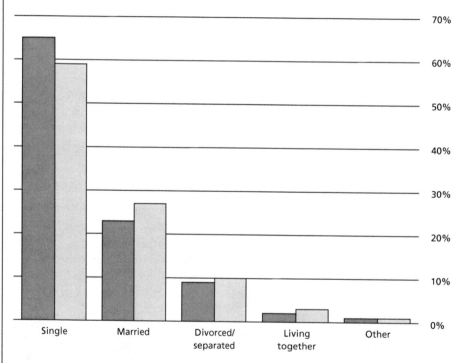

About a quarter (23 per cent) of the birth mothers were married compared with 27 per cent of the birth fathers.

As we shall see in the next chapter, there were striking differences when contrasting the above figures with the comparable data about the marital status of adoptive families, most of whom were married couples.

There were also significant differences in the age profile of the birth mothers classified according to their marital status. The lowest mean age at birth of child was found in the single mothers and those living with their partner outside marriage, with respective averages of 23 years 1 month and 21 years 10 months. In the married birth mothers, the mean age at birth of child was 27 years 5 months, which compared with a significantly higher mean (31 years 8 months) in the birth mothers described as "divorced or separated".*

Single mothers under the age of 18 years represented 11 per cent of the overall birth family sample. These very young birth mothers aged less than 18 years were of course more likely to have a single child at the time the Form E was completed when compared with the rest of the single birth mothers in the other age groups (see Figure 6.4 below).

KEY FINDING

The lowest mean age was found in the single mothers and those living with their partner outside marriage, with respective averages of 23 years 1 month and 21 years 10 months. In the married birth mothers, the mean age at birth of child was 27 years 5 months.

Figure 6.4

Number of birth children in the single birth mothers by age at birth of child

Note: Percentages of birth mothers within each age band. N=876 single mothers for whom data on age and number of children were available.
* Numbers of birth children in the legend refer to all children and include the adopted child(ren).

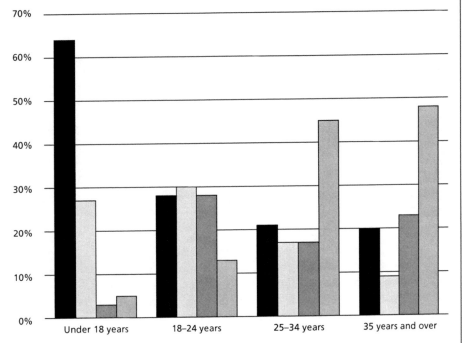

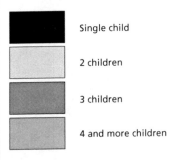

Single child

2 children

3 children

4 and more children

Nearly two-thirds (64 per cent) of the single mothers aged under 18 years had only one child, compared with 28 per cent of those aged 18–24 years and approximately a fifth of the older single birth mothers. Not surprisingly, the highest number of birth children was found in the mothers aged 35 years and over: 48 per cent of these single mothers had 4 children or more (including the adopted one(s)). Nearly a fifth (18 per cent) had more than 5 birth children.[†]

Single mothers with one child and aged under 18 years accounted for 7 per cent of all the birth mothers in the sample.[‡]

KEY FINDING

Single mothers under the age of 18 years represented 11 per cent of the overall birth family sample.

6.2.2 Occupation

The impact of socio-demographic factors such as unemployment, lone-parenthood or social deprivation on the numbers of children and families needing support from local authorities has long been established by research (Bebbington, 1976; Holman, 1980; Parker, 1983, p. 19; Bebbington and Miles, 1989).

The Department of Health has acknowledged that socio-cultural factors such as poverty, racism, poor housing or unemployment are likely to undermine parenting capacity (Department of Health, 1989).

* F=103.474 df 3 at p<0.01 (N=1,322 birth mothers for whom data concerning both martial status and age were available). Excluding 15 deceased birth mothers and 5 widows.

† χ^2=235.548 df 15 at p<0.01; Cramer's V=0.299 (N=876 single mothers for whom data on age and number of children were available).

‡ N=1,338 birth mothers with full details of age, marital status and number of birth child(ren)

It was therefore interesting to look at an overview of the occupational status of the birth parents whose children had left care for adoption during 1998/99. The results showed a very specific socio-economic profile of these parents: the most noticeable finding was that 89 and 68 per cent respectively of the birth mothers and fathers were not working at time of "best interest" decision (see Table 6.2 below).

Table 6.2

Birth parents' occupation at time of "best interest" decision

Note: As recorded on assessment material at the time of "best interest" decision (Standard Occupational Classification [SOC]). N=1,339 birth mothers (missing data for 109 mothers), N=952 birth fathers (missing=496). * "Not working" includes housewives in the birth mothers, as well as a tiny number of cases where the mother was described as "prostitute".

Occupation / situation	Birth mother		Birth father	
	N	%	N	%
Working	160	11	301	32
I-II: Professional, Managerial, Technical	11	1	16	2
III: Skilled	30	2	67	7
IV: Partly skilled	49	3	40	4
V: Unskilled	70	5	178	19
Not working	1,179	89	651	68
Unemployed	920	69	557	59
At home, not working*	170	13	18	1
Student	76	6	31	3
HM Prison	13	1	45	5
TOTAL	1,339	100	952	100

Of the small number of birth parents who did have an occupation, only a tiny minority (less than 2 per cent of both the mothers and fathers) were employed in professional, managerial and technical positions, while the vast majority were partly skilled and unskilled employees and workers.

6.3 Parental responsibility

This last section focuses on the issue of parental responsibility, bearing in mind that the issue of birth parents' agreement to the adoption plan was dealt with in Chapter 4. Looking at the extent to which birth parents had parental responsibility for the adopted child revealed significant differences between birth mothers and fathers.

Of the latter, only 27 per cent were described as legally responsible for the child, which compared with 91 per cent of the birth mothers.*

Cases where the birth mother did not have parental responsibility for the child included the small number of deceased birth mothers (about 1 per cent of the birth family sample) as well as the few cases where the child(ren) was subject to a freeing order at the time of completing the assessment Form E (about 2 per cent). To account for the remaining 6 per cent it must therefore be assumed that there was some misunderstanding on the part of those completing this part of the form; a small number of children were wards of court and others were subject to residence orders; neither of these would have removed the mother's parental responsibility but would have had the effect of limiting their ability to exercise it.

As explained in the introduction to this chapter, the information about birth fathers was scarce, particularly the details of parental responsibility and agreement to the adoption plan for the child(ren). However, it was interesting to note that there were differences in the extent to which birth fathers had

* Mothers: N=1,374 cases, missing information in 74 cases; Fathers: N=1,145 cases, missing=303.

agreed to adoption according to whether they had parental responsibility for the child(ren).

In those cases where details of agreement to the adoption were known, over half (51 per cent) of the birth fathers with no legal responsibility for the child(ren) were consenting to the adoption. This compared with 36 per cent of the fathers who were described as having parental responsibility.*

KEY FINDING

Over half of the birth fathers with no legal responsibility for the child(ren) were consenting to adoption, compared with 36 per cent of the fathers who had parental responsibility.

References

Bebbington, A (1976) *Policy Recommendations and the Needs Indicator for Social Service Provision for Children,* Discussion paper No 34, Personal Social Services Research Unit, University of Kent.

Bebbington, A Miles, J (1989) *The Background of Children who enter Local Authority Care,* The British Journal of Social Work, Vol. 19, No 5, October.

Department of Health (1989) *The Care of Children. Principles and Practice in Regulations and Guidance,* London, HMSO.

Holman, R (1980) *Inequality in Child Care,* Poverty Pamphlet No 26 (2nd edn.), London: Child Poverty Action Group.

Parker, R A (1983) *A Forward Look at Research and the Child in Care, A Report for the Social Science Research Council, Children in Care Panel,* Department of Social Administration, School of Applied Social Studies, University of Bristol, August.

* The above differences were statistically significant: $\chi^2=15.566$ df 1 at $p<0.01$; Cramer's V=0.146.

The adoptive parents

The last important area examined by the adoption survey was the characteristics of the adoptive families with whom the children were placed for adoption. Adoptive parents are an essential part of the "adoption triangle" (Reich and Batty, 1990) and there are numerous issues in relation to how local authorities respond to the changing profile of children needing adoption by recruiting adopters for children with special needs. These children include those with physical disability or health needs, those from black and minority ethnic backgrounds including mixed parentage, and children with siblings.

As explained in the introduction to this report, major changes in adoption have encouraged new thinking about the range of people who should be considered as prospective adopters. It is therefore important to draw a more accurate picture of the profile of families and individuals who come forward to adopt looked after children.

The data sets collected from the participating local authorities offered the opportunity to research this aspect of adoption practice, and allowed comprehensive examination of the adopters' profile, patterns of placement, and the adopters' expectations at the time of approval. Details of 1,448 adoptive families were obtained, which related to the 1,801 children in the study (see sample overview in Chapter 2).

In the first of the following sections we describe some broad characteristics of the adopters, and the composition of the adoptive family household. In the second section we concentrate on the adoption procedures, attendance at preparation groups, and time-scales between approval of adopters and placement of child(ren). Then we analyse some of the important requirements stated in the adopters' applications to adopt regarding the number, gender and needs of the child(ren).

7.1   The adopters' profile

This first section explores the characteristics of the 1,448 adoptive families in the sample with regard to the adopters' marital status, ethnicity, religious affiliation, occupation, and working hours. We then move on to analysing the composition of the adoptive family household.

7.1.1 Status of adopters

One important question to be answered from the data was the number of single adoptive parents. Previous studies have highlighted the strength of single-parent adoptive families, and there is research evidence of the specific contribution to adoption for looked after children by single adopters (Owen, 1999).

The extent of adoption by single parents

KEY FINDING

5 per cent of all the adopters were single.

KEY FINDING

4 per cent of all the children had been adopted by single adopters

Overall, the picture for the 1998/99 cohort of adopters for looked after children was predominantly one of couples. Adoptions by single people were relatively rare – single adopters accounted for only 5 per cent of the total. Of the 63 single adopters, a total of 59 (that is 92 per cent) were female.* There is no information about the number of lesbians and gay men who adopt children every year. As explained by Triseliotis *et al* (1997, pp.222–223):

---

* N=1,418 adopters; information was missing in 30 cases out of 1,448

Little is known about lesbian women and gay men who adopt. Again, these data are hidden in the studies of single parents, for surely some of them at least are lesbian or gay. Many of these adoptions are only nominally or legally single-parent adoptions, for there is often a partner forming a two-parent family.

However, in Owen's study (1999) of single parent adopters, all 30 single adopters in the study described themselves as single and without an adult partner. A total of 57 per cent of the single parents had never been married, 37 per cent were divorced or separated, while another 6 per cent were widows or widowers.

Single adopters and foster carers

Adoption by foster carers has been discussed in the preceding parts of this study (see in particular Chapters 4 and 5). Cases of parents adopting their foster child(ren) amounted to 13 per cent of the 1,448 adoptive families in the sample.

One important finding was the correlation between single parent and foster carer adoption. As can be seen from Figure 7.1 below, adoptions by the children's foster carers were significantly over-represented in the group of single adopters.

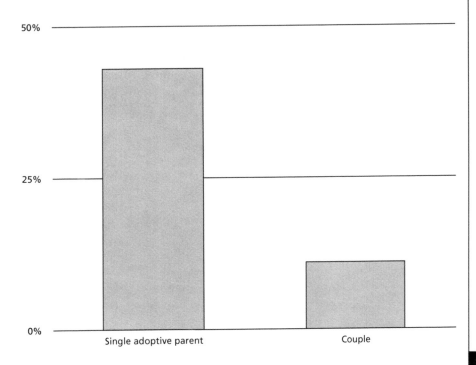

Of the single parents who had adopted during 1998/99, a total of 43 per cent were already fostering the child(ren), as opposed to only 11 per cent of the couples.*

Variation in single parent adoption across types of local authority

There were also some significant differences in the overall proportion of single adopters with regard to the type of recruiting agency (see Figure 7.2).

Single adoptive parents were found in a higher proportion across the inner London boroughs, where they accounted for nearly a quarter (24 per cent) of

* χ^2=52.029 df 1 at p<0.01; Phi=0.197.

KEY FINDING

Of the single adopters, 92 per cent were female.

KEY FINDING

57 per cent of the single parents were unmarried, 37 per cent were divorced or separated, while another 6 per cent were widows and widowers.

KEY FINDING

Cases of parents adopting their foster child(ren) amounted to 13 per cent of all adoptive families in the sample.

Figure 7.1

Percentage of single adopters and adoptive couples who were adopting their foster child(ren)

Note: Percentages of adopters by marital status adopting their foster children.
N=1,418 adopters; information missing in 30 cases.

KEY FINDING

Adoptions by the children's foster carers were significantly over-represented in the group of single adopters: 43 per cent as opposed to 11 per cent of the couples.

KEY FINDING

Single adoptive parents were found in a higher proportion across the Inner London Boroughs (24 per cent), compared with percentages varying from 2 to 6 per cent in the other types of agency.

Figure 7.2

Percentage of single adopters by types of recruiting agency

Note: N=1,418 adopters; information missing in 30 cases.

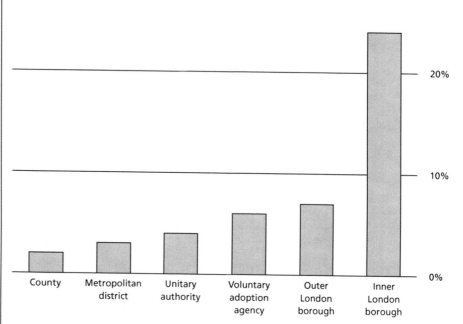

all adoptive families. This figure compared with percentages varying from 2 to 6 per cent in the other main types of agency.*

While there was some variation across the main types of local authorities, there was no evidence of a similar variation between statutory and voluntary adoption agencies. The proportions of single adoptive parents were very similar when comparing adopters recruited by local authorities with those recruited by agencies in the voluntary sector.†

The children's profile by type of adopter

Was there a special contribution to adoption for looked after children by single adopters? Did children adopted by single parents have a distinctive profile with regard to their characteristics, previous care histories, and special needs? To answer these questions, the children in the sample were compared on some important characteristics according to whether they had been adopted by single parents or couples. Details are summarised in Table 7.1 below, together with all relevant statistics.

It is important to stress that, unlike most of the data in this chapter, the following figures had to be based on the children sample in order to take account of cases where placement had been secured for more than one child.

Comparing the children's characteristics revealed some differences between the two main types of adoption considered for this part of the analysis. Significant variation in the children's profile were found in terms of the child's ethnic background, age at adoption, placement history, and, to a lesser extent, health problems (see Table 7.1).

On the other hand, no differences were observed in the children's profile with regard to the balance of gender, the presence of siblings, legal status at completion of Form E, developmental problems and/or learning difficulties, and the extent of both physical and sexual abuse (see all relevant Chi-Square statistics in Table 7.1).

* χ^2=56.631 df 5 at p<0.01; Cramer's V=0.200.
† χ^2=2.798 df 2 p=0.247 n.s.

Table 7.1

The profile of children placed with single adopters and couples

Characteristics	Percent of children placed With single adopters	With couples	χ^2	df	Sig.	Cramer's V
Gender						
% of boys	44	51	1.432	1	0.231	n.s.
% of girls	56	49				
TOTAL	100					
Ethnicity						
% white	66	92	151.907	2	p<0.01	0.294
% black*	9	7				
% mixed parentage	25	2				
TOTAL	100					
Sibling groups						
Placed alone	72	63	2.553	1	0.110	n.s.
Placed with siblings	28	37				
TOTAL	100					
Age at adoption						
% under 1 year	–	7	54.968	4	p<0.01	0.177
% 1–4 years	33	60				
% 5–9 years	49	28				
% 10–14 years	18	4				
% 15 years and over	–	1				
TOTAL	100					
Health problems						
% moderate	12	10	7.852	2	0.020	n.s.
% serious	12	5				
Placement history						
% single placement	16	39	29.516	5	p<0.01	0.130
% multiple placements	84	61	6.699	2	0.035	n.s.

Note: N=1,761 children. Percentages within each category of adopters. * "Black" refers to African Caribbean, African and Asian. **Records of "possible" and "definite" sexual abuse were grouped together in order to avoid small counts.

KEY FINDING

A quarter of the children placed with single adoptive parents were of mixed-parentage. This compared with only 2 per cent of those adopted by couples.

KEY FINDING

40 per cent of the African, African-Caribbean and Asian children had been adopted by single adopters, against 6 and 3 per cent of the mixed-parentage and white children respectively.

KEY FINDING

Children adopted by single parents were considerably older at the time of making the adoption order: two-thirds of those children were aged 5 years and over, as opposed to a third of those adopted by couples.

Children of a minority ethnic background were found to be over-represented in the group of children adopted by single parents. A quarter (25 per cent) of the children placed with single adoptive parents were of mixed parentage. This compared with only 2 per cent of those adopted by couples. As we shall see in the next section, single adopters themselves were more likely to be of a minority ethnic origin.

Figure 7.3 below contains the same information, but uses the child's ethnic origin as the main group of reference. As can be seen, a total of 40 per cent of the African, African-Caribbean and Asian children had been adopted by single adopters, against 6 and 3 per cent of the mixed parentage and white children respectively.

The children's age at adoption in Table 7.1 also reveals sizeable differences between the children adopted by single parents and those adopted by couples. Children adopted by single parents were considerably older at the time of making the adoption order, with over two-thirds (67 per cent) of these children aged 5 years and over. In contrast, only a third (33 per cent) of the children adopted by couples were found in these age groups.*

It should be borne in mind, however, that cases of foster carer adoptions were significantly over-represented in the single parents. Preceding considerations regarding the profile of carers adopting their foster child(ren) have shown substantial differences in the age profile of the children, with those adopted by their foster carers being significantly older (see Chapter 4).

* Using age at first entry into care or age at placement with adopters gave similar results.

Figure 7.3

Adoption by single parents by ethnic origin of child: a comparison between black, mixed parentage and white children

Note: N=1,761 children. Percentages of single parent adoptions within each ethnic category. "Black" refers to African, African-Caribbean and Asian.

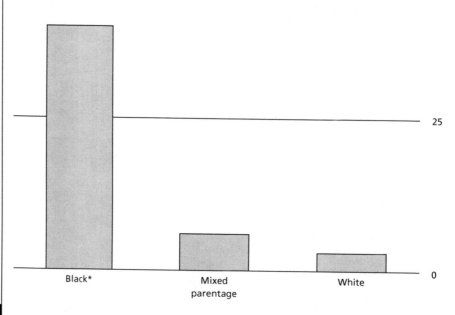

Black*	
Mixed parentage	
White	

A third area of variation was the child's placement history. Consistent with the above findings concerning the age profile of the adopted children, the study found that children adopted by single parents were more likely to have had a greater number of placements; of these children, only 16 per cent had a single placement before the adoptive placement as opposed to nearly 40 per cent of those adopted by couples.

Lastly, there were some differences, albeit of a lower magnitude, in terms of the child's medical condition. Severe health problems were found to be over-represented in the children placed with single adopters (12 per cent as opposed to 5 per cent in the children adopted by couples). Caution should be exercised, however, given the lower level of statistical significance for these findings.

7.1.2 Ethnicity

The vast majority (89 per cent) of adopters in the 1998/99 cohort were couples where both partners were white. Couples where both applicants were either black or of mixed-parentage represented approximately 2 per cent of the total sample (see Table 7.2).

However, an analysis of the ethnic origin of adopters according to their status showed that, while most couples (93 per cent) consisted of two white adopters, a significant proportion (34 per cent) of single adopters were drawn from ethnic minorities, with most being of mixed parentage. Single parent adopters of African, African-Caribbean and Asian backgrounds amounted to only 4 per cent of all single parents, and less than 1 per cent of all adopters.

7.1.3 Religion

As can be seen from Table 7.3, approximately 6 in 10 of the adopters in the 1998/99 cohort were Church of England; 15 per cent were Catholic; and 16 per cent were of another Protestant denomination. Only very few (about 6 per cent) adopters were described as having no particular religious affiliation. This should perhaps be compared with 25 per cent of the birth mothers and nearly a third (30 per cent) of the birth fathers who were

	N	% of total sample	% within categories of adopters
Single white	42	3	66
Single black*	3	0	4
Single mixed parentage	19	2	30
Total single adopters	64	5	100
Couple both white	1,259	89	93
Couple one white + one mixed parentage	26	2	2
Couple one white+ one black*	35	2	3
Couple both mixed parentage	1	0	0
Couple one black* + one mixed parentage	1	0	0
Couple both black*	32	2	2
Total couples	1,354	95	100
TOTAL	1,418	100	

Table 7.2

Ethnicity and status of adopters

Note: N=1,418 adopters (missing information in 30 cases); * "Black" refers here to African, African-Caribbean and Asian

similarly described as "no religion" (see relevant section in preceding chapter).

Of the single adopters, 10 per cent had no religious affiliation and 16 per cent were Catholic. The largest religious groups found amongst single adoptive parents were Church of England (39 per cent) and other Protestant (34 per cent).

KEY FINDING

Of the single adopters, 10 per cent had no religious affiliation and 16 per cent were Catholic. The largest religious groups found amongst single adoptive parents were the Church of England (39 per cent) and other Protestant (34 per cent).

	Adopter # 1 N	%
None	158	6
Church of England	1,610	60
Catholic	400	15
Other Protestant*	430	16
Other religious denomination**	69	3
TOTAL	2,667	100

Table 7.3

Adopters' religious affiliation

Note: N=2,667 adopters for whom the information was available. * "Other Protestant" not Church of England, Methodist; ** "Other religious denomination" includes Jehovah's Witness, Jewish, Muslim, Sikh, Mormon, Hindu and Seventh Day Adventist, which were all found in small numbers in the adopter sample.

Looking at patterns of religion in the adoptive couples showed that over half (51 per cent) of them consisted of two Church of England partners, 11 per cent of two other Protestants, and 6 per cent of the couples comprised two Catholic adopters.

KEY FINDING

Over half of the couples consisted of two Church of England partners, 11 per cent of two other Protestant, 6 per cent two Catholic adopters.

7.1.4 Occupation

The occupational data about the adoptive families in the sample showed some interesting patterns, which could be contrasted with those derived from the analysis of the birth parents' socio-economic background. Unfortunately, the assessment Form F, through which the information about adoptive parents was collected, did not request specifically that social workers record the occupation of adopters, and only contained the indication of the number of hours worked per week.

The following findings about the adopters' occupational profile were derived from a subset of 430 adopters for whom occupational data were available through the alternative questionnaires that were sent to the group of local authorities who were not using BAAF Form F (see details of data collection in Chapter 2). Caution should therefore be exercised when analysing these findings, although there is no obvious reason to believe that proportions should vary significantly across the other agencies in the study.

KEY FINDING

Nearly 70 per cent of all single adopters were working full-time, another 23 per cent were working part-time, and the remaining 9 per cent were not working.

* N=1,293 adopters for whom data were available in both partners.

One striking difference with the comparable figures for the birth families was the significantly lower level of unemployment in the adoptive families. While 59 and 69 per cent of the birth fathers and mothers respectively were

Table 7.4

Occupation of adopters

Note: N=789 adopters with full data.

	Adopter # 1	
	N	%
Unemployed	14	2
Not working (housewives, retired, student)	109	14
I & II: Professional, Managerial, Technical	303	38
III: Skilled occupation	143	18
IV: Partly skilled occupation	150	19
V: Unskilled	70	9
TOTAL	**789**	**100**

KEY FINDING

Approximately 4 in 10 of all adoptive parents were employed in professional, managerial and technical occupations, and a similar proportion were found in skilled and partly skilled positions.

KEY FINDING

Of the single adopters, over a third had a professional, managerial and technical occupation, whilst another 14 per cent were found in skilled and partly skilled occupations.

unemployed, only 2 per cent of the adoptive parents were found in a similar situation. Approximately 4 in 10 of all adoptive parents were employed in professional, managerial and technical occupations, and a similar proportion were found in skilled and partly skilled positions.

Of the single adopters, over a third (36 per cent) had a professional, managerial and technical occupation, whilst another 14 per cent were in skilled and partly skilled occupations. Nearly 7 in 10 (69 per cent) of all single adopters were working full-time, another 23 per cent were working part-time, and the remaining 9 per cent were not working at the time of completing Form F.* It should be noted that this was at the initial completion of Form F; many adopters noted they they would alter working hours/ arrangements after adoption.

A total of 42 per cent of the couples consisted of two adopters working full-time, and another 40 per cent comprised one partner working part-time and one working full-time. Cases of couples with one partner not working amounted to 16 per cent of all the couples in the study.†

7.1.5 Children in the adoptive family

Together with the profile of the adoptive parents, it was of interest to look at the composition of the adoptive family household, the child's position in the family and the age gaps between children. Some children are placed in established families with birth children but we need a more accurate picture of the extent of placement for looked after children with "childfree" adopters.

Adoption by "childless" parents

The number of adoptive parents who had children, either full,‡ step or adoptive and/or fostered children was investigated. Figures are summarised in Table 7.5, and include all children whether living in the adoptive family household or elsewhere at the time of completing Form F.

Table 7.5

The number of adopters with full, step and adopted / fostered children

Note: N=1,418 adopters. Figures include all children, either living with adopters or elsewhere. Also included are a tiny number of deceased children.

	% of adopters with full birth children		% of adopters with step children		% of adopters with adopted/fostered children	
	N	%	N	%	N	%
No children	1,122	79	1,306	92	1,050	74
1 child	164	12	57	4	270	19
2 children	80	6	35	3	72	5
3 and more	51	4	20	1	26	2
TOTAL	**1,418**	**100**	**1,418**	**100**	**1,418**	**100**

* N=35 adopters for whom information was available.

† N=997 adoptive couples with full data.

‡ "Full" is used to describe chilldren born to the adopter or to both adopters if a couple.

As can be seen from Table 7.5 above, nearly 8 in 10 (79 per cent) of the adopters had no full birth children. Only a small number (8 per cent) had step-children. A quarter (26 per cent) of the adopters had at least one adopted or fostered child.

This information was cross-tabulated in order to identify the number of adopters who had no birth children, either full or step, as well as to isolate those who only had adopted and/or fostered children. These results are shown in Figure 7.4 below.

7 The adoptive parents

KEY FINDING

Nearly three quarters of the adopters had no birth children, either full or step. A fifth had only adopted and/or fostered children, whilst another 15 per cent had full birth children but had never adopted or fostered before.

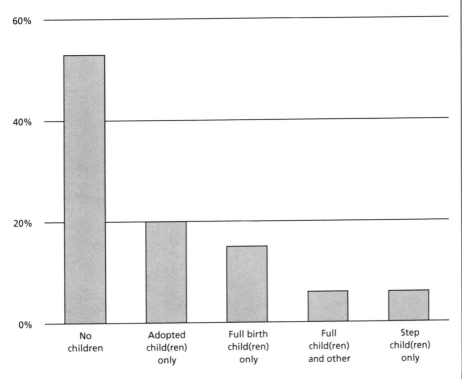

Figure 7.4

Percentage of adopters with full, step and adopted/fostered children

Note: N=1,418 adopters. Figures include all children, either living with adopters or elsewhere. Also included are the tiny number of deceased children.

The above calculation revealed that, overall, 73 per cent of the 1998/99 adopters were "childless" adopters i.e. they had no birth children, either full or step. This figure includes adoptive parents in the sample who had only adopted and/or fostered children (20%), while another 15 per cent had full birth children but had never adopted or fostered before.

Using the above classification also helped identify significant differences between single adoptive parents and couples. While the proportion of adopters with no children was very similar across both groups, there was some variation in the percentages of adopters with full and adopted children. Single parents were found to be more likely to have full birth children (33 per cent as opposed to 14 per cent of the couples). In contrast, adopters who had already adopted and/or fostered children were over-represented in the couples: 20 per cent against 6 per cent of the single parents.

KEY FINDING

Single parents were more likely to have full birth children: 33 per cent as opposed to 14 per cent of the couples.

KEY FINDING

Adopters who had already adopted and/or fostered children were over-represented in the couples: 20 per cent against 6 per cent of the single parents.

The composition of the adoptive family household

Another important issue that could be addressed from the survey data was the composition of the adoptive family household. So far, the analysis has included all the adopters' children, whether living at home or elsewhere. In this section, we concentrate exclusively on the children living with the adoptive parents at the time of adoption.

Figure 7.5 below contains the information concerning the presence of other children in the adoptive family household. Data were classified according to

* χ^2=25.271 df 4 at p<0.01; Cramer's V=0.133. Adopters with step-children only were all couples.

four main types of children living with adopters: full birth children, step, adopted and foster children. Percentages refer to the proportion of adoptive parents who had at least one child type living with them when completing Form F.

Figure 7.5

Percentage of adopters who already had children in their household at time of application by category of child

Note: N=1,418 adopters (missing information in 30 cases).

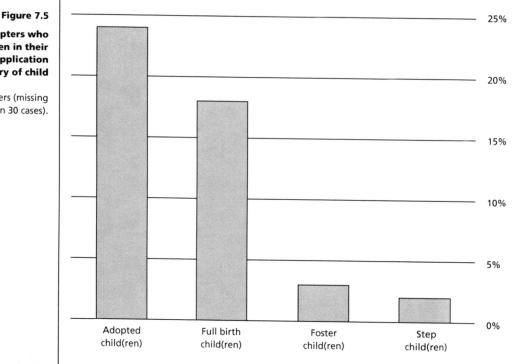

Figure 7.5 shows a quarter (24 per cent) of the adoptive parents in the 1998/99 cohort had already at least one adopted child living with them when they were assessed for adoption. Nearly a fifth (18 per cent) had at least one birth child. Cases of adopters fostering one or more children were in the minority (3 per cent), as were cases where step-children were still living at home with adopters (2 per cent).

KEY FINDING

More than half of the adopters in the sample had no children living with them. Another fifth had only adopted children living with them, and only 15 per cent had full birth children at home.

Table 7.6

Children already living at home with adopters at time of placement

Note: N=1,418 adopters (missing information in 30 cases). For the sake of clarity, categories with very small counts were regrouped as follows: adopted and foster children = foster children; step and adopted child(ren) = adopted children; full, adopted and foster child(ren) = Full and adopted child(ren); Full and step child(ren) = Full child(ren) only.

	N	%
No children living at adopter's home	823	58
Adopted child(ren) only	297	21
Full child(ren) only	210	15
Full and adopted child(ren)	35	2
Step-child(ren) only	20	1
Full and foster child(ren)	17	1
Foster child(ren)	16	1
TOTAL	**1,418**	**100**

As can be seen from Table 7.6 above, more than half (58 per cent) of the adopters in the sample had no children living with them at the time of completing Form F. Another fifth (21 per cent) of the adopters had only adopted children living with them, whilst 15 per cent had only full birth children at home.

There was a significant variation in the proportion of established families when looking at the number of children adopted during 1998/99. As can be seen from Figure 7.6 below, children placed with siblings were more likely to be adopted by families with no established children: a total of 84 per cent of the sibling groups were placed with such families, as opposed to 52 per cent of the children adopted individually.*

KEY FINDING

Children placed with siblings were more likely to be adopted by adoptive families with no established children: 84 per cent of the sibling groups were placed with such families, as opposed to 52 per cent of the singletons.

* χ^2=99.055 df 3 at p<0.01; Cramer's V=0.265.

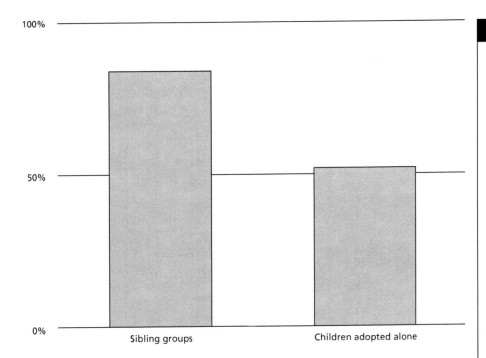

Figure 7.6

Proportion of adopters who had no children in their household, by number of children

Note: N=1,407 adopters (missing information in 41 cases).

The age structure of the adoptive family

There are important issues in respect of the age profile of the children in the already established adoptive homes, and the age gap between these children and those who were subsequently adopted during 1998/99.

Beginning with the age profile of the children in the 595 adoptive families with established children, the study found that the average age of the youngest child (at times the only one) was 7 years 11 months, ranging from 4 months to a maximum to 25 years 6 months. For the oldest child in the adoptive family, the mean age at time of completing Form F was 9 years 10 months, with a fairly similar range between 4 months and 26 years.

The above figures refer to all children living with adopters, and therefore include adopted and fostered children (see preceding section).*

Table 7.7 contains summary figures for the age position of the children adopted during 1998/99 within the established adoptive families. We look at the subset of children adopted individually, for whom it is possible to calculate the age position within the established adoptive family.

KEY FINDING

The average age of the youngest child in established families was 7 years 11 months, the oldest 9 years 10 months.

Children adopted individually	N	% of all families adopting a single child	% of established families adopting a single child
Youngest child in the household	514	46	96
Between youngest and oldest	16	1	3
Oldest child in the household	7	1	1
Total established families	537	48	100
No children in the household	577	52	
TOTAL	**1,114**	**100**	

Table 7.7

Age position of the adopted child in the adoptive family household: children placed individually

Note: N=1,114 adoptive families who adopted a single child during 1998/99

As mentioned earlier, 52 per cent of the children adopted individually had been adopted by families without children living at home. In another 46 per cent of the cases, the adopted child was the youngest child in the adoptive family household. Concentrating exclusively on the single children placed with established families, nearly all (96 per cent) of these children were the youngest child in the adopters' home.

KEY FINDING

Nearly all (96 per cent) of the children placed with established families were the youngest child in the adopters' home.

* N=584 adoptive families with full data available. Information missing in 11 adoptive families with established children.

7.2 Adoption procedures

This second section focuses on some important aspects of the adoption procedures in relation to the adoptive families. The emphasis is more specifically on the number of adopters recruited by voluntary adoption agencies, the age of adopters at the time of approval for adoption, the length of time between approval and placement of child(ren), as well as the adopters' specific requirements regarding placement.

7.2.1 Adopters' recruiting agency

Details of inter-agency placements and the contribution by the voluntary sector to adoption for looked after children were presented at length in Chapter 4. In this first section, the information is simply presented from the perspective of the adoptive families. Figure 7.7 below contains the proportion of adopters recruited by external agencies.

KEY FINDING

In 75 per cent of the cases, adopters had been found within the local authority area, and in another 10 per cent they had been recruited by another local authority.

Figure 7.7

Adopters' recruiting agency

Note: N=1,448 adoptive families

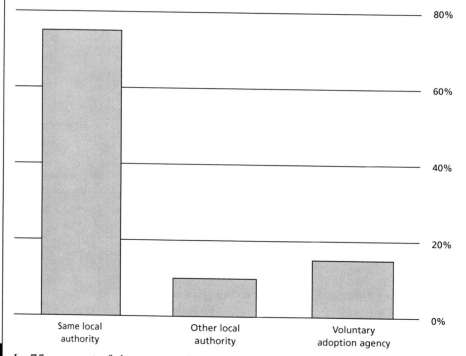

In 75 per cent of the cases, adopters had been found within the local authority area, and in another 10 per cent they had been recruited by another local authority. Recruitment of adopters by agencies in the voluntary sector amounted to 15 per cent of the adoptive family sample.

KEY FINDING

Recruitment of adopters by agencies in the voluntary sector amounted to 15 per cent of the adoptive family sample.

7.2.2 Age of adopters at approval

The mean age of single adopters when approved for adoption by the relevant agency was 40 years 4 months, while it was 37 years 8 months for the couples who had adopted during 1998/99.* Foster carer adopters were considerably older with a mean age at approval of 42 years 4 months for single adopters and 43 years 6 months for married foster carer adopters.

KEY FINDING

The mean age of single adopters at approval was 40 years 4 months; it was 37 years 8 months in the couples.

In the single adopters, the minimum age at approval in the sample was 30 years 4 months, and the maximum 55 years 5 months. For the couples, the minimum was 24 years 1 month, the maximum 59 years 1 month.[†]

Adoptive parents were clustered into four different age categories (see Figure 7.8). As can be seen, there were no single adopters below the age of

---

* These differences were statistically significant: $F=13.705$ df 1 at $p<0.01$. N=1,368 adopters with full data.
† N=1,368 adopters with full data; "Age of couple" refers to mean age of partners.

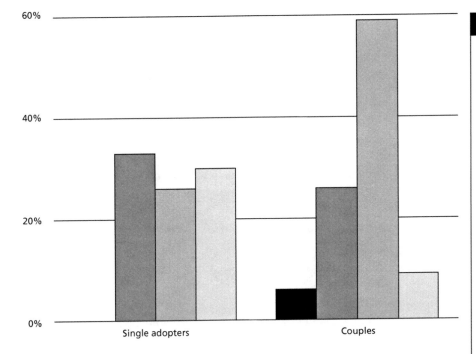

Figure 7.8

Age of adopters when approved for adoption by single adopters and couples

Note: N=1,868 adopters with full data. Percentages within each group of single adopters and couples.

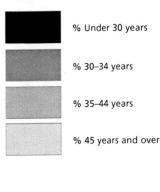

% Under 30 years

% 30–34 years

% 35–44 years

% 45 years and over

30 years, and the single adoptive parents were fairly equally distributed across the three other main age bands considered for the analysis.

Nearly 6 in 10 (59 per cent) of the couples were aged 35–44 years when approved for adoption by the relevant agency. A tiny proportion (6 per cent) were couples under 30 years of age. Compared with the single adopters, only 9 per cent of the couples were found in the 45 years+ age group (against 30 per cent of the single parents).

Over 4 out of 10 (41 per cent) of the foster carer adopters were aged 35–44 at approval, and another 42 per cent were aged 45 years and over. Only 6 per cent of the foster carers who had come forward to adopt their foster child(ren) were under the age of 30 when approved as adopters.

7.2.3 Age gap between adopters and children

On average, the age gap between adopters and the adopted child(ren) at the time of placement was 35 years 7 months, ranging from 21 to just over 54 years. No significant differences were found in terms of single adopters and couples.*

7.2.4 Time between approval and placement

One important issue in relation to the process of recruiting adopters for looked after children is the length of time between approval by the agency and placement of child(ren) with the adoptive family.

There was some variation in the total length of time that elapsed between approval and placement. On average, placement of child(ren) had been achieved within 9 ½ months in the whole 1998/99 sample of adoptive families.†

No significant variation was found across the main types of recruiting agency. Nor were differences statistically significant when looking at the average waiting time before placement for the adopters recruited by local authorities and for those recruited by voluntary adoption agencies.‡

KEY FINDING

There were no single adopters below the age of 30 years, and the single adoptive parents were fairly equally distributed across the other age bands.

KEY FINDING

Nearly 6 out of 10 couples were aged 35–44 years when approved for adoption.

KEY FINDING

The age gap between adopters and the adopted child(ren) at the time of placement was 35 years 7 months.

KEY FINDING

Placement of child(ren) had been achieved within 9 ½ months following approval.

* F=0.028 df 1 p=0.827 n.s. (N=1,400 adopters with full data).

† N=1,387 adopters (missing information in 61 cases)

‡ Type of agency: F=1.928 df 5 p=0.087 n.s.; adopters' recruiting agency: F=4.425 df 2 p=0.012 n.s.

KEY FINDING

Foster carers coming forward to adopt their foster child(ren) had significantly shorter periods of waiting between approval and placement: 4 months as opposed to 10 months for the families adopting children unknown to them.

Foster carers coming forward to adopt their foster child(ren) had significantly shorter periods of waiting between approval and placement: on average, foster carers had children placed with them within a 4 month period, as opposed to 10 months for the families adopting children unknown to them.* The above differences are largely accounted for by the very specific nature of the process of turning a foster placement into an adoptive one.

When taking into account the impact of this particular group of foster carer adoptions, and bearing in mind these were over-represented amongst single adopters, there were no significant differences in terms of the time waiting for placement between single adopters and couples.†

7.2.5 Preparation groups and adoption allowances

The data collected from participating local authorities through BAAF Forms E and F helped identify cases where adopters had attended preparation groups, as well as cases where it was suggested that the adoptive family should benefit from an adoption allowance. The former piece of information was available from Form F, whilst indications of the latter were found on Form E.

Preparation groups

KEY FINDING

The vast majority (87 per cent) of adopters had attended preparation groups.

Of the whole 1998/99 cohort of adopters, a large majority (87 per cent) had attended preparation groups.‡ It should be noted that, in most cases, this meant taking part in a substantial number of meetings prior to the placement of child(ren).

Significant differences in the extent to which the adoptive parents had joined such groups were found between foster carers adopting their foster children, and the rest of the adopters in the sample (see Figure 7.9 below).

While most (91 per cent) of the adoptive families who had adopted children unknown to them had attended preparation groups, only 60 per cent of the foster carers adopting their foster child(ren) had done so.**

Figure 7.9

Preparation groups: a comparison between foster carers and the "new families"

Note: N=1,389 adopters with full data. Percentages of adopters who attended preparation groups within each category of adoptive family. * "New families" refer to adopters adopting children unknown to them.

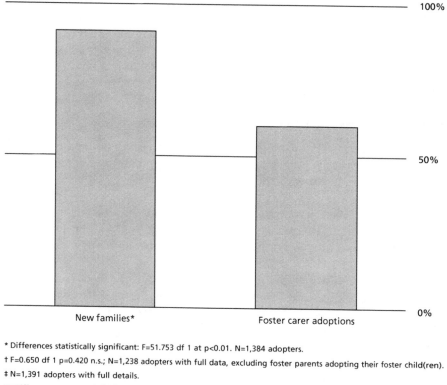

New families*   Foster carer adoptions

* Differences statistically significant: F=51.753 df 1 at p<0.01. N=1,384 adopters.

† F=0.650 df 1 p=0.420 n.s.; N=1,238 adopters with full data, excluding foster parents adopting their foster child(ren).

‡ N=1,391 adopters with full details.

** Differences were statistically significant: χ^2=135.310 df 1 at p<0.01; Cramer's V=0.312

When controlling proportions of adopters attending preparation groups for cases of foster carer adoptions, no significant differences were found between single adopters and couples.*

Adoption allowances

Some caution should be exercised when looking at figures for adoption allowances. The process of collecting data through Form E only allowed investigation of the number of cases where an adoption allowance was planned by the relevant case worker at time of completing Form E, and therefore did not allow for any subsequent change. Neither was it possible to assess the extent to which these allowances were actually granted to the adoptive families at a later stage of the process.

Indications of the need for an adoption allowance were found in nearly a fifth (18 per cent) of all adoptive families in the sample. Whilst the extent to which adoption allowances were suggested did not vary significantly across the main types of local authorities,[†] there was empirical evidence of a greater likelihood of cases of foster carer adoptions to be associated with financial support for adoptive parents through adoption allowances.

Of all adoptions by foster carers, 40 per cent were described as needing an adoption allowance, as opposed to only 15 per cent in the rest of the sample.[‡]

As can be seen from Figure 7.10 below, single parents adopting children unknown to them were also more likely to be the beneficiary of an adoption allowance when compared with the couples in the relevant group of "new families". Of the single parents, 53 per cent were described as adopting child(ren) who may imply the need for financial support, while it was only the case in 14 per cent of the couples.

In contrast, no differences were found in the group of foster carers adopting their foster child(ren), with similar proportions of cases where financial support would be desirable: 39 per cent in the single foster carers and 45 per cent in the couples within the relevant group for comparison.**

7 The adoptive parents

KEY FINDING

91 per cent of the "new" adoptive families had attended preparation groups, compared with 60 per cent of the foster carers adopting their foster child(ren).

KEY FINDING

Indications of the need for an adoption allowance were found in nearly a fifth of all adoptive families in the sample.

KEY FINDING

40 per cent of the adoptions by foster carers were described as needing an adoption allowance, as opposed to only 15 per cent in the rest of the sample.

KEY FINDING

Over half of the single parents had adopted child(ren) who may imply the need for financial support, compared with 14 per cent of the couples.

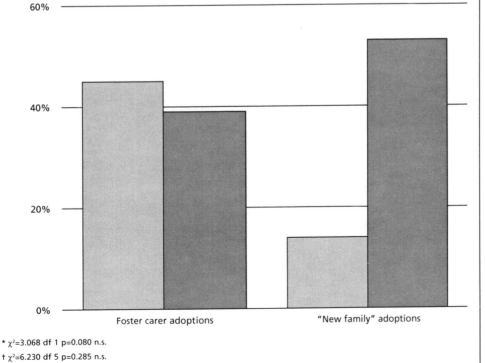

Figure 7.10

Adoption allowances: foster carers and the "new families", single adopters and couples

Note: N=1,370 adopters with full data. Percentages of adopters adopting children for whom an adoption allowance would be desirable. * "New families" refer to adopters adopting children unknown to them.

Couples

Single adopters

* χ^2=3.068 df 1 p=0.080 n.s.
† χ^2=6.230 df 5 p=0.285 n.s.
‡ χ^2=58.652 df 1 at p<0.01; Cramer's V=0.207
** New families: χ^2=39.855 df 1 at p<0.01; Phi=0.182; Foster parents: χ^2=0.273 df 1 p=0.601 n.s.

7 The adoptive parents

KEY FINDING

Adoptions with financial support were slightly over-represented in the boys (24 per cent), children looked after under care orders (23 per cent), those placed with siblings (29 per cent) and those aged 5 years+.

KEY FINDING

Over a third of the children described as having developmental and/or learning difficulties were cases where an adoption allowance was planned.

KEY FINDING

The need for financial support by the authority was found in 43 per cent of the children with a severe medical condition, and 55 per cent of the children described as sexually abused.

The need for an adoption allowance to be granted by the authority was defined in relation to the children's needs rather than the adopters' particular circumstances. Clearly, the characteristics of the child(ren) to be placed with adopters were very likely to include factors accounting for the need for an allowance to be granted by the relevant local authority. The distribution of cases of adoption with allowances was analysed across the main groupings of children in terms of their gender, ethnicity, age, legal status and special needs and revealed significant differences.

Adoptions with financial support were found to be slightly over-represented in the boys (24 per cent as opposed to 18 per cent of the girls), the children looked after under care orders (23 per cent against 14 per cent of those under voluntary agreements), as well as in the children placed as part of a sibling group (29 per cent compared with 16 per cent of those adopted individually) and those aged 5 years+ at the time of "best interest" decision by the agency.*

The child's needs were found to exert an even more significant influence on whether the option of granting an adoption allowance had been considered. Over a third (35 per cent) of the children described as having developmental and/or learning difficulties were cases where an adoption allowance was planned. The need for financial support by the authority was found in 43 per cent of the children with a severe medical condition (as opposed to 20 per cent in the rest of the sample), and 55 per cent of the children described as sexually abused.†

In contrast, other characteristics such as the child's ethnic origin or congenital risks had no clear impact on the extent to which local authorities planned to grant adoption allowances.‡

7.2.4 Considerations regarding placement

The final important area of interest to be addressed from the survey data was that of the adopters' views about adoption, and the profile of the child(ren) they were prepared to adopt. Two points must be made here. Firstly, it is important to stress that the information was drawn from details of specific preferences and/or reservations regarding placement of child as expressed by the adopters at the time of completion of Form F.

Secondly, the information contained in the "considerations" section of Form F may not always reflect the adopters' views about the desirable profile of the child(ren), but may, at times, relate to the process of preparing to adopt a specific child or group of children, and therefore reflect these children's circumstances and needs rather than those of the adopters.

Considerations recorded on Form F include the number, gender, age and special needs of the children whom the adopters were prepared to adopt. We examine these aspects in turn in this last section, and make a tentative evaluation of the extent to which the profile of the looked after children adopted during 1998/99 corresponded with earlier "expectations" by their adoptive parents.

---

* Relevant Chi-Square statistics were as follows: gender: $\chi^2=9.694$ df 1 at p<0.01; Phi=0.076; legal status: $\chi^2=14.311$ df 1 at p<0.01; Phi=0.092; sibling groups: $\chi^2=42.169$ df 1 at p<0.01; Phi=0.157; age at "best interest" decision: $\chi^2=101.310$ df 4 at p<0.01. Cramer's V=0.244.

† All differences statistically significant. Developmental difficulties: $\chi^2=44.652$ df 1 at p<0.01; Phi=0.162; medical condition: $\chi^2=27.076$ df 2 at p<0.01; Cramer's V=0.126; sexual abuse: $\chi^2=28.938$ df 2 at p<0.01; Cramer's V=0.130.

‡ Ethnic origin: $\chi^2=0.719$ df 2 p=0.698 n.s.; congenital risks: $\chi^2=0.136$ df 1 p=0.712 n.s.

Number of children considered by adopters

As can be seen from Table 7.8 below, over half (56 per cent) of the 1998/99 adopters were initially considering adopting a single child, while 39 per cent were prepared to accept a group of two siblings.

Number of children considered by adopters	N adopters	% of adopters
Single child	791	56
2	544	39
3	57	4
4 and more	18	1
TOTAL	1,410	100

Table 7.8

Number of children considered by adopters at time of assessment

Note: N=1,410 adopters with full data (missing information in 39 cases)

Taking account of foster carer and single parent adoptions revealed significant differences, particularly in the group of foster carers coming forward to adopt their foster child. In the latter category, nearly all (96 per cent) of the single parents were considering adoption for a single child, as opposed to 65 per cent of the couples who were fostering the child(ren) prior to adopting them. The difference between single adopters and couples were not found to be significant in the "new families" adopting children unknown to them.*

KEY FINDING

Over half of the adopters were initially considering adoption for a single child, and 39 per cent were prepared to accept a group of two siblings.

In Table 7.9 below, the information concerning the adopters' preferences was cross-tabulated with the actual number of children adopted. There was strong empirical evidence that, in most cases, the number of children placed with adopters corresponded to the number that had been indicated in the "consideration" section of their assessment form.

KEY FINDING

In the group of foster carers, nearly all (96 per cent) of the single adopters were considering adoption for a single child, as opposed to 65 per cent of the couples.

Number of children considered by adopters	How many children were placed (actual placement)					Total
	Single child placement	Group of 2 siblings	Group of 3 siblings	Group of 4 siblings	Group of 5 siblings	
Single child	99 (784)	1 (7)				100 (791)
2 children	58 (317)	42 (226)	0 (1)			100 (544)
3 children and more	20 (15)	33 (25)	35 (26)	8 (6)	4 (3)	100 (75)

Table 7.9

Number of children considered by adopters and number of children adopted

Note: N=1,410 adopters with full data (missing information in 39 cases); Row percentages within each category of number considered (counts in brackets)

Nearly all (99 per cent) of the adopters who had indicated their preference for a single child placement had only one child placed with them for adoption, bearing in mind that children placed individually represented by far the largest group of children within the 1998/99 cohort (see Chapter 4).

Interestingly, only 42 per cent of the adopters who were initially prepared to consider adoption for a group of two siblings had two children placed with them, while over half (58 per cent) had a single child, due to the over-representation of children to be adopted individually.

Overall, there were only a tiny number of cases where the number of children placed with adopters was larger than the one specified on Form F. This should not be taken to mean that the adopters' expectations in terms of placement were met in the majority of the cases. As explained earlier, it is

KEY FINDING

Nearly all (99 per cent) of the adopters who had indicated their preference for a single-child placement had only one child placed with them for adoption.

KEY FINDING

42 per cent of the adopters who were initially prepared to consider adoption for two siblings had two children placed with them. Over half had a single child.

* Foster carer adoption: Single adopters / couples: χ^2=10.712 df 2 at p<0.01; Cramer's V=0.245; "New" families: Single / couples: χ^2=2.863 df 2 p=0.269 n.s. N=1,408 adopters in the sample. The small numbers of adopters considering adoption for 3, 4 and 5 children were grouped together.

very likely that a substantial number of adopters' Form F were completed following the identification of a child or group of children needing adoption, and therefore primarily reflected the children's needs and circumstances.

Gender of the child(ren)

As can be seen from Figure 7.11, over three-quarters (76 per cent) of the adoptive families in the study were prepared to consider adopting either a boy or a girl. Another 24 per cent of the adopters had indicated a "gender preference", 62 per cent of these preferences being for a girl.

Figure 7.11

Gender of children considered by adopters

Note: N=1,366 adoptive families with full data; percentages of adopters.

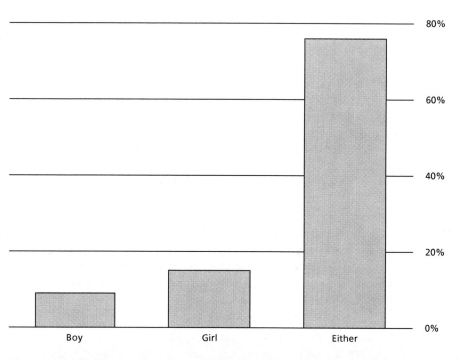

Placement of sibling groups consisting of both genders made it difficult to assess with accuracy the actual level of correspondence between pre-placement considerations by adopters and the actual gender profile of the child(ren) placed with them. As can be seen from Table 7.10, nearly all (99 per cent) of the adopters considering a boy had a boy placed with them. A total of 90 per cent of the adopters who were initially favouring adoption of a girl adopted a girl.

Table 7.10

Gender of child considered by adopters and gender of the adopted child(ren)

Note: N=1,695 children with full data; row percentages within each category of gender considered by adopters (counts in brackets)

Gender of children considered by adopters	Gender of children adopted (actual placement)		Total
	Boy	Girl	
Boy	99	1	100
	(134)	(1)	(135)
Girl	10	90	100
	(22)	(202)	(224)
Either	53	47	100
	(705)	(631)	(1,336)

An important aspect of the above finding is the over-representation of children placed individually with adopters who had indicated a "gender preference". Of these, 87 and 82 per cent respectively of the adopters considering a boy or a girl had a single child placed with them, compared with only 59 per cent of the adoptive parents who had no particular preference with regard to the gender of child.

* These differences were statistically significant: χ^2=75.838 df 2 at p<0.01; Cramer's V=0.212.

However, controlling for the number of children placed for adoption and concentrating on the subset of children placed individually confirmed that 7 per cent of the adopters who preferred a girl had a single boy placed with them, and therefore were not cases where the adoptive parents had adopted a group of siblings of both genders.

Age of the child(ren)

The third area that was given consideration by adopters was that of the age of the child. The data collected from Form Fs contained a variety of age ranges, and there was a great deal of variability in the way the information had been recorded by case workers. For the purpose of the analysis, the numerous age bands described at the time of completion of Forms Fs were clustered into four main groups which are described in Table 7.11 below.

Age range considered by adopters	N	% of all adopters	% of cases where age was indicated
0–1 year	143	10	11
2–4 years	553	38	42
5–9 years	537	37	41
10 years+	72	5	6
Total specified	1,304	90	100
Not specified	143	10	
TOTAL	1,448	100	

The age of the child had been given no specific consideration by 10 per cent of the adopters. Of the cases where the "age preference" was indicated, only 11 per cent were adopters considering adoption of babies and infants up to one year of age. A total of 42 per cent of the adoptive parents were prepared to consider a child up to the age of 4, and another 41 per cent had indicated a preference for a child up to the age of 9. Adopters considering adoption for older children aged 10 years+ were in the minority (6 per cent of the overall sample of adoptive parents).

As explained earlier, cases of placements of sibling groups were likely to have a distorting impact on the assessment of whether adoption had met the adopters' expectations with regard to the age profile of the child(ren). Adoptive parents looking for adoption of a young baby may consider the possibility of adopting an older sibling.

Figure 7.12 contains the distribution of the adopted children's age at placement according to the four main age bands considered by adopters at the time of completing Form F. For the sake of clarity, children were grouped into four comparable clusters of age at placement with adopters.

Almost all (94 per cent) adopters considering young children aged 0–1 year had a child within that age range placed with them. In contrast, nearly three-quarters (72 per cent) of the adoptive parents who were prepared to accept a child up to 4 years had a placement of a younger child under the age of 2 years, whilst another 27 per cent had a placement of child(ren) within the 2–4 years age band.

Overall, people who adopted children above the upper limit of the age band they were considering in the first place accounted for a tiny proportion (less than 2 per cent) of the sample. Controlling these findings for the number of children placed, particularly by excluding cases where placement had been

KEY FINDING

The age of child had been given no specific consideration by 10 per cent of the adopters.

Table 7.11

Age range of child(ren) considered by adopters at the time of completing Form F

Note: N=1,448 adoptive families; percentages of adopters within each group of age considered for adoption

KEY FINDING

11 per cent were adopters considering adoption of babies and infants up to one year of age. 42 per cent were prepared to consider a child up to the age of 4, and 41 per cent had indicated a preference for a child up to the age of 9.

KEY FINDING

The vast majority (94 per cent) of adopters considering young children aged 0–1 year had a child within that age range placed with them. In contrast, nearly three quarters of those prepared to accept a child up to 4 years had a placement of a younger child under 2 years, and another 27 per cent had children within the 2–4 years age band.

KEY FINDING

Overall, cases of parents adopting children above the upper limit of the age band they were considering accounted for a tiny proportion (less than 2 per cent) of the adopters sample.

Figure 7.12

Age of child at placement by age range considered by adopters at completion of Form F

Note: N=1,304 adopters with full data. Percentages of children within each age band considered by adopters

% of children 0–1 year

% of children 2–4 years

% of children 5–9 years

% of children 10 years+

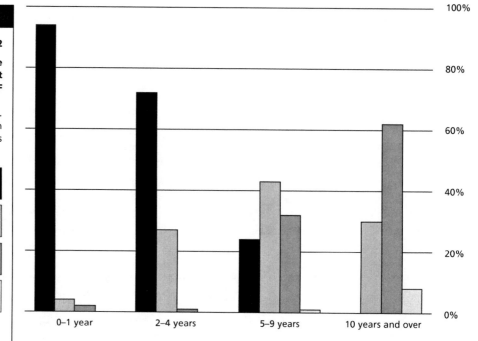

achieved for groups of siblings, revealed no significant variation from the above patterns.

The child's legal situation

Together with the above socio-demographic characteristics of the child, adopters were invited to indicate their views over a series of difficulties or needs which a child needing a new family may have. These difficulties included "complex legal situations" such as cases where care orders were planned but not yet granted, and cases of contested adoptions in the absence of freeing orders.

It was evident from the data collected through Forms F that the issue of legal proceedings had not been addressed in a systematic manner. There was no indication of the adoptive family's views about possible delay entailed by complex legal proceedings in a quarter (24 per cent) of the adopters sample.

> **KEY FINDING**
>
> Of the cases where information was recorded, 89 per cent were adopters prepared to adopt a child with a complex legal situation.

Of the cases where the information was recorded, 89 per cent were adopters prepared to adopt a child with a complex legal situation. Unfortunately, the information concerning the child's legal situation was not sufficient to explore further the issue of legal proceedings.

The child's special needs

> **KEY FINDING**
>
> Only a minority (13 per cent) of the adopters were prepared to accept a child with a mental disability.

Lastly, there were a series of considerations regarding adoptive placement for children with special needs or difficulties. The design of Form F allowed investigation of the adopters' acceptance of children who may potentially have special needs in terms of their health condition, educational needs, and previous experience of abuse.

> **KEY FINDING**
>
> 4 in 10 of the adopters in the sample were not prepared to accept a child with a physical disability.

The adopters' views about children with special needs

A total of six areas of need are covered in the assessment Form F. These include physical disability, mental disability, medical condition, special educational needs, sexual abuse and physical abuse. For each of these categories of need, adopters are asked to indicate whether they are prepared to accept a child with the relevant type of problem. Adopters are given three possible categories of answer: "yes", "no" and "limited/ambivalent".

> **KEY FINDING**
>
> 38 per cent were prepared to accept a child who would need special educational support.

There were limitations on the data collected in response to the above questions on Form F, particularly the definition of "needs" used by the relevant social worker when conducting the interviews with prospective adopters. However, it was interesting to compare the adopters' attitudes towards the various categories of needs they were asked about at time of assessment. The results of this procedure are summarised in Figures 7.13 and 7.14 below.

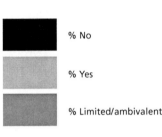

Figure 7.13

Adopters prepared to accept children with special needs: mental disability, physical disability, special educational needs, and medical condition

Note: N=1,250 adopters with full data. Percentages of all adopters.

- █ % No
- ▓ % Yes
- ▓ % Limited/ambivalent

Beginning with the child's special needs, the study found that only a minority (13 per cent) of the adopters were prepared to accept a child with a mental disability. Only 14 per cent were "ambivalent" with regard to that particular category, and a negative response was given by nearly three-quarters (73 per cent) of the adopters, by far the highest level of "refusal".

Similarly, more than 4 in 10 (44 per cent) of the adopters in the sample were not prepared to accept a child with a physical disability. A third (35 per cent) were prepared to consider a child with "limited" physical impairment.

Adoptive parents were less concerned about adopting a child with special educational needs (15 per cent did not wish to) while nearly half (48 per cent) of the adopters were in the "limited/ambivalent" category; 38 per cent were prepared to accept a child who would need special educational support.

Lastly, the level of "refusal" was found to be significantly lower in respect of the child's medical condition, with only 12 per cent of the adopters indicating they would not be prepared to adopt a child with health problems, against 47 per cent who would and another 40 per cent who would be prepared to accept a child with "limited" (i.e. moderate) health problems.

Turning to the child's history of abuse, there was a substantially higher level of acceptance amongst the adopters in the sample with very few of them being ambivalent in respect of sexual and physical abuse. Over two-thirds (69 per cent) of the adoptive parents stated their readiness to adopt a child with a history of sexual abuse. For children who had been subjected to physical abuse, the figure was as high as 83 per cent.

Overall, considering all the above categories of needs, a total of 12 per cent of the adopters were prepared to accept a child with 5 needs or difficulties

KEY FINDING

Adopters were mostly prepared to adopt a child with health problems; only 12 per cent indicated they would not be prepared to do so against 47 per cent who would, and another 40 per cent who would be prepared to accept a child with "limited" health problems.

KEY FINDING

Over two-thirds of the adoptive parents stated their readiness to adopt a child who had a history of sexual abuse. For children who had been subjected to physical abuse, the comparable figure was as high as 83 per cent.

KEY FINDING

Overall, 12 per cent of the adopters were prepared to accept a child with 5 problems and more. 23 per cent of the adoptive parents had answered "no" to all six categories of problems when interviewed.

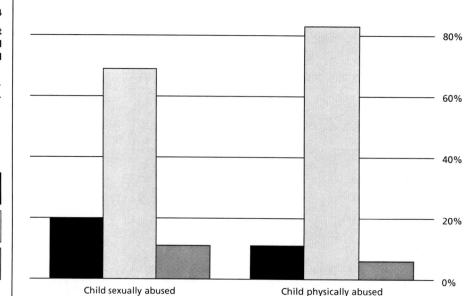

Figure 7.14

Adopters prepared to accept children who were sexually and physically abused

Note: N=1,250 adopters with full data. Percentages of all adopters.

% No

% Yes

% Limited/ambivalent

Child sexually abused

Child physically abused

and more. At the other end of the scale, 23 per cent of the adoptive parents had answered "no" to all six categories of problems when interviewed.

Patterns of placement for children with special needs

The above anaysis raised the question of whether the relevant local authority had managed to meet the expectations of adoptive parents with regard to placement for children with special difficulties and/or a history of abuse.

Again, we should be cautious when exploring the data made available through Forms E and F as there may be some important variation in the interpretation of the extent and nature of a child's needs by relevant case workers. There are undoubtedly a variety of other important aspects to the process of matching children and adopters, such as subsequent changes in the adopters' views when presented with a possible match, which account for some of the discrepancies that were found in the following parts of the analysis.

In this last section, we concentrate on the adopters who had strong reservations about adopting children with a specific type of need, or a previous history of abuse. For each of the six main categories of difficulties, we look at the proportions of adopters who had expressed their wish not to accept a child with such a need, and determine whether or not this was the outcome.

Let us begin with the child's medical condition. None of the adopters who had initially rejected adoption of a child with a medical condition had a child with severe health problems placed with them. A total of 11 per cent of these adopters had adopted a child with "moderate" health problems (see Chapter 3 for the definitions used for the analysis of the children's special needs). Over three-quarters (76 per cent) of the children described as having serious medical problems were placed with adopters prepared to accept such children.

Only 1 per cent of the adopters who were not initially prepared to consider adoption of a sexually abused child had adopted children for whom there was an indication of "definite" sexual abuse. A total of 89 per cent of the small group of children described as sexually abused had been adopted by

KEY FINDING

Over three-quarters of the children described as having serious medical problems were placed with adopters prepared to accept such children.

KEY FINDING

Only 1 per cent of the adopters who were not initially prepared to consider adoption for a sexually abused child had adopted children for whom there was an indication of "definite" sexual abuse.

KEY FINDING

89 per cent of the group of children described as sexually abused had been adopted by parents who had expressed their confidence in dealing with that particular type of difficulty.

parents who had expressed their confidence in dealing with that particular type of difficulty in their adopted child(ren).

A similar conclusion applied to the analysis of placement of physically abused children: 87 per cent of these children had been adopted by parents who initially indicated that they would, while another 11 per cent had been placed with adopters who had "ambivalent" feelings. On the other hand, less than 1 per cent of the adopters who had explicitly refused to adopt a physically abused child had a child with such difficulty placed with them.

In contrast, and keeping in mind the limitations imposed on the data by the lack of clear definitions for the categories of needs, the analysis found that 11 per cent of the adopters who had previously rejected the possibility of adopting a child with special educational needs had actually adopted a child described as having developmental and/or learning difficulties. Nearly a third (31 per cent) of the children listed with developmental problems and/or learning difficulties had been placed with adopters who had said they were not prepared to adopt such children at the time of completing Form F.

References

Reich, D Batty, D Burnell, A Fitsell, A (1990) *The Adoption Triangle*, London: BAAF.

Triseliotis, J Shireman, J and Hundleby, M (1997) *Adoption: Theory, Policy and Practice*, London: Cassell.

Owen M (1999) *Novices, Old Hands and Professionals: A study of single parent adoptions*, London: BAAF.

KEY FINDING

87 per cent of the physically abused children had been adopted by parents who were prepared to accept them, while another 11 per cent had been placed with adopters who had "ambivalent" feelings.

KEY FINDING

Nearly a third of the children listed with developmental problems and/or learning difficulties had been placed with adopters who were not initially prepared to consider a child with such problems.

Conclusion

Felicity Collier
Chief Executive, BAAF

The current study relates to adoptions finalised during 1998/9, the first year of two new initiatives introduced by the Department of Health. The first was the introduction in August 1998 of Local Authority Circular 98 (20), *Adoption – achieving the right balance*, which required local authorities to consider adoption much more proactively for looked after children. The second, linked to the Quality Protects programme, announced in September 1998, required local authorities to maximise the use of adoption for looked after children in order to promote stable attachments and to reduce placement moves. It seems unlikely, however, that the Quality Protects Management Action Plans, required to be in place from 1 January 1999, would have had an impact on the adoptions which were finalised during the year 1998/99 and which are the subject of this study.

BAAF's previous study, *Focus on Adoption* (Dance, 1997), provided base line information about the age, ethnicity, and marital status of adopters in 1995 and also information about the adoption of minority ethnic children, sibling groups and disabled children, and the respective contributions of the voluntary and statutory sectors. *Children Adopted out of Care* (Ivaldi, 1998) provided important statistics about the length of time taken to place looked after children for adoption in 1996, their care history and age profile. It is therefore possible to consider changing patterns in the three years between those studies and the current study and their relevance for contemporary adoption.

It is also an opportune time to consider the implications of these new findings for the development of adoption policy and practice, particularly in the light of the recommendations included in the Prime Minister's Review, which at the time of going to press, are subject to consultation.

Adopted children

One of the most significant findings in this study is that the overall duration of care has reduced from three years eight months in 1996 to three years 1 month in 1999. This is a very encouraging trend and does demonstrate that progress is being made to reduce delay – although clearly there is still a long way to go. It is also very interesting to note that the average age at which children, who later left care through adoption, started to be looked after, has reduced by eight months – from one year ten months to one year two months. While there has been a gradual decrease in the age of children starting to be looked after generally, this sharp drop would certainly suggest that planning is improving for younger children who cannot return to their birth families – hence the drop in age at entry. This trend continues with the average age of children at adoption falling from five years six months in 1996 to four years three months in 1999. This would seem to combine the fact that the children were younger when they started to be looked after with the shorter time span between entry and adoption.

It is important that we exercise caution in considering the implications of these findings – it could be that increased activity in adoption work has led to younger children being identified for adoption at the expense of older children, although, given the inevitable time lapse before such policy changes result in action, it seems likely that the change will also reflect firstly, the younger age of children starting to be looked after and secondly, the prevalence of more entrenched birth family problems. It is also possible that greater insistence by some courts on clear plans has helped local authorities to crystallise their thinking about adoption.

The study is unable to identify whether drug and alcohol misuse by birth parents has made a significant difference to the age of entry into care of adopted children although it is generally considered that more infants have come into care as a result of such problems. The pattern of other reasons for coming into care is very similar to previous patterns with four out of ten adopted children taken into care because of neglect or abuse.

There is no difference in the frequency of children returning home – four out of five children who have been adopted have had one continuous period of being looked after prior to adoption.

While over a third of children have had a single placement prior to placement for adoption, a worryingly higher number appear to have had multiple changes of placement with 29 per cent having four placements or more. Of particular concern was the fact that 44 per cent of infants between one and twelve months had had four or more changes of placement, although it should be noted that 50 per cent of these infants had had at least one return home which would have been included in the overall number of moves. Nevertheless, we are clearly looking at some very young infants, separated from their birth families and experiencing change and discontinuity of care, who reach adoptive families after a significant time lapse. This does have to be questioned given our increased knowledge about the importance of the infant's development in the first year of life, and would indicate a tighter timescale for considering adoption where investment in work with the birth family is not successful.

The information about average timescales from entry into care to "best interest" decision, and from "best interest" decision to placement and then to adoption, is very valuable at a time when the Government appears committed to setting targets for adoption services for each part of the adoption process. However, the study also identifies a number of factors which impact on the average. Certain groups of children experience greater delay at each step of the process – some of these issues will be explored in greater detail later in this chapter. However, the impact of age at entry into care, ethnicity, health problems or special needs, and legal status are so significant that it would seem very difficult to set realistic targets which would apply to all children, without adding a distorting factor which could act as a disincentive to providing adoption for certain children, who might be over-represented (at least in relation to ethnicity) in some parts of the country. Policy makers will wish to study the findings in Chapter 5 very carefully.

Foster care and adoption

It should be noted that the average time scales for each stage in the adoption process are strongly influenced by small groups of children who take a very much longer time. Adoption by foster carers has significant influence on average time scales with children being almost twice as old at entry into care and over two years older than the rest of the adopted children in the sample at the time of "best interest" decision.

It is significant that the average age of children adopted by foster carers is six years three months and this does suggest that foster carer adoption may be regarded as the last resort for children, perhaps after lengthy exploration of alternative placements. The low number of foster carer adoptions raises questions about the commitment of agencies to supporting such adoptions. It is interesting to compare this to the US experience where 65 per cent of all children adopted out of care in 1998 were adopted by foster carers. The other dimension, of course, which may contribute to this great difference in practice, is the availability of adoption allowances – 40 per cent of the foster carers adopting were identified as requiring an allowance. The practice in the USA is very different with almost all families being granted very substantial allowances which only fall slightly short of foster care allowances. It is certainly of concern if children are being moved, from foster carers to whom they are securely attached, for financial reasons.

The results of this study suggests that further work is needed urgently on examining policy in relation to how foster carer applications to adopt should be viewed and whether they should be actively encouraged where the child has a strong attachment. Considerable potential benefits could ensue for many children if they could have a permanent legal status with their carers which would recognise the life-long commitment made by the new families.

It is also relevant that, of the very small number (5 per cent of the sample) of single adopters who adopted, 43 per cent of these were already fostering the child; 42 per cent of the foster carer adopters were 45 years and over at the time of approval for adoption compared with only 10 per cent of the new adopters. Such findings suggest that agencies would need to embrace a flexible response to age and to marital status in order to promote more foster carer adoptions.

Another observation about foster carer adopters is that 27 per cent of all the mixed parentage children adopted transracially were adopted by their white foster carers and these children were among the longest in care before the adoption decision was made. It is likely that it was the length of time with the same foster carers that will have persuaded the agency to support adoption rather than moving the child to an ethnically matching adoption placement.

A possible policy implication might be that foster carer adoption should be considered as a possibility as soon as it becomes evident that a child is unable to return home. Should it always be considered before decisions are made to seek a "new" adoptive family? This should not have to lead to an increase in transracial placement if agencies were proactive in recruiting black or mixed heritage families to their pool of foster carers.

Minority ethnic children

The findings in relation to black and mixed parentage children certainly give rise to some concerns. The overall percentage of minority ethnic children out of all adoptions is 10 per cent – although the SSI Survey undertaken in 1999 found that 17 per cent of the children waiting for adoption were from minority ethnic backgrounds.

We do not have information about the children for whom adoption was the plan who are not adopted. Another study by BAAF (2000) demonstrated that the proportion of children from minority ethnic backgrounds referred to BAAF's child placement services is very high – 26 per cent of all accepted child referrals – and many of these received very few responses from potential adopters. However, it would be reasonable to assume that children are currently referred to national services because of agencies' concern to locate the most appropriate families for them; the actual number of children featured between 1998 and 1999 was 374 children. If all these children, let alone others who are not referred to BAAF, were placed for adoption then we would be seeing at least double the number of minority ethnic children adopted since this number would constitute 20 per cent of the sample.

It should be noted, however, that the proportion of children adopted is generally fairly similar to the proportion of the local minority ethnic population – so that 40 per cent of children adopted in Inner London are from minority backgrounds compared to 34 per cent of all children under 18 in Inner London as detailed in the Local Authority Key Indicators published by the Department of Health. Of course we know that that some groups of minority ethnic children are more likely than their counterparts in the general population to be admitted into care. It would be very useful if local authorities monitored the ethnicity of children for whom adoption is the plan and compared this with the ethnicity of children in the authority's care for more than two years.

Seventy-three per cent of all the minority ethnic children were of mixed parentage with only 19 per cent (17 children) of African-Caribbean or African background and 8 per cent (12) Asian children. There were significant differences at each stage of the process – adopted minority ethnic children were much younger when they started to be looked after, particularly African and African-Caribbean children who were 4 months old on average compared to 1 year 2 months for the whole sample. The African-Caribbean children were very unlikely to have returned home. All the minority ethnic children were far less likely to have developmental, medical or learning difficulties than the white children. Could a reason for this difference be that older minority ethnic children and those with special needs were unlikely either to be referred for adoption or, alternatively, less likely to achieve adoption?

One of the areas of greatest concern relating to minority ethnic children was the time taken between entry into care and "best interest" decision and "best interest" decision to placement. In particular, children starting to be looked after under 1 month under voluntary agreement waited a little less than 6 months for the best interest decision if they were white or of mixed parentage, but 12 months if they were black* – such delay for a small infant must be unacceptable. The length of delay is consistent for each stage of the process for infants which also suggests that it took longer to identify adoptive parents – possible lessons from these findings are complex. Could it be that the delay in reaching the best interests decision, is an effect of institutional racism? Perhaps there are communication difficulties with some social workers and relinquishing mothers, or a paralysis that sets in over concerns about contacting extended family members? Perhaps agencies delay in reaching the best interests decision because they fear that there will be a difficulty in identifying suitable adopters? We do not, of course, have the answers to these questions but it must be right that we ask them as we strive to provide an equal service to all children, including those of an ethnic minority.

It also took three times as long for black infants under six months to be placed for adoption and twice as long for black infants aged 6–12 months. For children over 30 months, delays were as significant for mixed parentage as black children – 14 months for both groups compared to 9 months for white children in the same age category. The delay in achieving placement indicates the importance of agencies having access to a national recruitment pool and for agencies putting more resources into the recruitment of minority ethnic adopters. The fact that minority ethnic children were also more likely to be placed on an inter-agency basis and that voluntary adoption agencies found over a quarter of the families, mainly in the secular agencies, is also helpful information. It was worrying to see that ethnicity was not identified on Form E as a matching issue for all children and it was noteworthy that

* "Black" refers to African-Caribbean, African and Asian.

transracial adoption seemed to be more likely to take place when this had not been highlighted. Given the requirement in the Children Act 1979 to take issues of "race" into account, this is surely unacceptable practice.

The percentage of transracial adoptions at just over 20 per cent of minority ethnic children overall was quite small, with only 2 per cent of black children adopted transracially compared to 28 per cent of mixed parentage children (remembering that a quarter of these were adopted by foster carers). The proportion of children adopted transracially has been remarkably consistent since 1995, when approximately 24 per cent of children were adopted transracially. While the placement of choice will always be an ethnically matching family, it is vital that we know if minority ethnic children are disproportionately represented amongst those children with an adoption plan who are never adopted. In that case it may be necessary to consider the capacity of white families to parent black and mixed parentage children if there is still a shortage of families which reflect the child's heritage when a national register is in place. It is also clear that priority must be given to recruitment campaigns targeted at minority ethnic communities.

Sibling groups

Children seemed to be placed with their siblings where there was a best interest decision for this to occur – 37 per cent of children were placed with siblings. However, 80 per cent of adopted children had birth siblings and although it must be recognised that some siblings may have never lived together, these findings also indicate the need to examine the basis on which decisions are made to separate siblings. It also raises questions about the degree to which agencies concentrate on maintaining links for these separated siblings – certainly such separations have implications for adoptive families who may need to facilitate contact and therefore may need post-adoption support, including financial assistance, to help them manage this.

Children placed together, as siblings, were also slightly more likely to be white. Could it be that fewer minority ethnic adopters are able to afford to adopt larger groups of siblings due to their lower incomes compared to the majority ethnic population and also have smaller living accommodation? This would clearly indicate the need for more creative support packages for families willing to adopt.

It is interesting that children placed for adoption are often part of very large families. It is not known from the study whether some of the siblings were born after the adopted child left the home, but given the time lag before adoption this seems likely in some cases. More adopters, at least at the time when they first applied to be adopters, were willing to take siblings, and larger groups of siblings, than those who eventually had siblings placed with them. Could it be that local authorities would prefer to use their own adopters and will therefore place single children with them rather than share the families more widely so that they can be linked with children elsewhere in the country? Do panels restrict the number of children families are approved for, although they may have indicated they would be prepared to take a sibling group?

Age of children

The fact that only 21 per cent of children were placed over the age of 5 years raises serious questions about messages currently given in adoption recruitment campaigns calling for adopters to come forward to adopt older children. On the other hand, it may be that there are significant numbers of older children for whom "best interest" decisions have been made who never reach adoption because adopters are not available. It is vital that we have accurate information about this because otherwise there will be enthusiasm about promoting the message that there are younger children waiting for adoption when it may be that the older children waiting simply are not adopted. (Indeed, in 1998/9 BAAF featured 589 children aged 6 to 15 in *Be My Parent* – 62 per cent of all children featured – and 210 children in this age group were referred to BAAFLink – 43 per cent.)

These findings also emphasise the need for agencies to be clear what their needs are so that local recruitment campaigns will give the right message. However, it is also important to take into account the profile of children waiting nationally for new families so that agencies can respond appropriately to families who would meet the needs of children elsewhere.

Special needs

For the first time we have clearer information about the incidence of special needs: 40 per cent of children overall had developmental delay, learning difficulties, a medical problem or hereditary risks (some of them having more than one). This underlines the vital importance of post-adoption support for the families who adopt these children but also emphasises the complex challenges which many adopters will face.

It was of concern that many of the adopters seemed unwilling, at least at the time of initial referral, to consider children with a range of special needs although in fact many of them later adopted such children. This might indicate ignorance by prospective adopters about the kind of children in need of families and also has implications for social workers about the point at which they discuss these issues. Information about children needing adoptive homes should be given at the start of the application process and also during the assessment and preparation of adopters.

It is generally thought unwise to ask adopters to consider children outside the range they might feel confident about parenting. There are implications here for the importance of providing effective post adoption support and for monitoring outcomes.

Influence of legal proceedings

Unfortunately, the survey did not identify how many children had been the subject of orders freeing them for adoption. Therefore, conclusions cannot be drawn as to the influence of the use of freeing orders on the timing of adoption proceedings.

Since the majority of children (77 per cent) were subject to care orders before they were adopted, it is possible to speculate to some degree on the impact of the care proceedings on the achievement of the local authority adoption plan. The duration of care proceedings themselves has been a matter of concern. In 1995, for example, the average length of time between the commencement of proceedings and the beginning of the final hearing for care proceedings in the county court was 43 weeks, and in the magistrates family proceedings courts between 25 and 30 weeks (Lord Chancellors Department 1994/5).

If the cases in the survey are typical (and there is no reason to suppose that they are not) decisions about the future of children concerned, and in particular the implementation of any decision to place for adoption, would inevitably have been delayed pending the outcome of the care proceedings. Children subject to emergency protection or interim care orders are still "looked after" as defined by the Children Act, and their care careers start as soon as one of these orders is made. The local authority concerned, however, will be constrained in its ability to implement an adoption plan until the granting of a full care order. The need for better co-ordination of decision making by courts and local authorities has been emphasised by both the Children Act Advisory Committee (1997) and the Department of Health (see, for example *Adoption: achieving the right balance*, LAC(98) 20) but difficulties inevitably persist, as outlined in the Report of the *Prime Minister's Review of Adoption* (2000), paragraphs 3.34–3.43. Nevertheless, the fact that there has been some reduction in the time spent by children in care prior to implementation of the adoption plan suggests that some progress may have been made in addressing these difficulties.

Disruptions

Only 2 per cent of the children placed for adoption had experienced a previous adoption placement – this seems very small and may offer some evidence about low disruption rates or, more probably, suggests that children who have experienced an adoption breakdown are unlikely to be adopted subsequently.

Birth families and adopters

The new information about the birth families of the adopted children presented in this study is very complex and could have significant social policy implications. The vast majority of birth mothers and fathers were not working at the time of approval of the child for adoption and, where they were doing so, were almost all in partly skilled or unskilled occupations. While the marital status of over two-thirds of the birth mothers was single, this does not of course preclude the fact that many of them may have been living with partners, or with their children's father. The fact that so many fathers do not have parental responsibility and that no information was available about the background of these fathers is more worrying. It is possible that agencies make less effort to find out about the background of the birth father when he does not have parental responsibility, thus potentially denying children subsequently, knowledge about his identity, and also making it impossible to explore his views, and those of the paternal extended family, about the adoption plan.

Of the older birth mothers (over the age of 25), nearly 50 per cent had 4 or more children. Family support services clearly need to target the economically disadvantaged and unemployed mothers with large families. Previous smaller studies of looked after children have found a high degree of poverty and unemployment among the parents of children coming into care. It was perhaps surprising that the birth parents were not younger, with the average age being 25, dispelling myths that the children of teenage mothers were more likely to end up being placed for adoption. Birth parents were much more likely to be of African or African-Caribbean background than of mixed parentage, and it would seem that the mixed parentage children placed for adoption were first generation mixed parentage.

In contrast, the adopters presented a very different picture. Only 5 per cent of adopters were single – therefore the vast majority of children born to single parents were adopted by married couples. This suggests that social workers still favour traditional family structures. Given the shortage of adopters for many children, and the time taken to locate adopters for those children later adopted and, more importantly, the concern that many children are never adopted for whom there is a plan for adoption, it is surely short-sighted not to encourage more single adopters to come forward. As stated earlier, single adopters often seem to be asked to take on the children with the most potential difficulties, children for whom it was more likely that an adoption allowance was under consideration. Surprisingly, 43 per cent of the single adopters were the children's foster carer which meant that the proportion of single "new" adopters out of all "new" adopters was considerably smaller.

Adopters were also significantly older than birth parents with an average age of nearly 38 – this is very consistent with the findings of BAAF's previous study of voluntary agency adoptions (Ivaldi, 2000) and must finally dispel the myth that adopters have to be under the age of 35.

All adopters provided information about their religion affiliation and only 7 per cent described themselves as having no religion. Nearly half of birth parents either described themselves as having no religion or the information was missing on the forms. This absence of information was even higher in relation to information about the children. In an increasingly secular society it would seem that many social workers do not ask about religious affiliation even though it is a requirement under the Adoption Act 1976. Adopters, of course, would complete the information themselves on the application form. It is suggested that there may be implications for attention to these issues in the training of social workers.

In class and employment terms, there is also a massive difference between birth families and adopters – only 2 per cent of adopters were unemployed and 55 per cent were in social classes 1 to 3, with 39 per cent in 4 and 5. Over a third of single adopters had professional, managerial and technical occupations and nearly 70 per cent were working full time (at the time the approval was agreed). Such information may be reassuring to middle class adopters who believe they are disadvantaged in the assessment process by social workers looking for "working class" families. On the other hand, given the backgrounds of the vast majority of the children adopted and the shortage of adopters, it would surely make sense to recruit more families from a wider social base.

The low percentage of married couples where adoption allowances were initially considered (14 per cent) may reflect the income levels of most of the adoptive families – single parents were much more likely to receive adoption allowances. If a wider range of families are to be encouraged to come forward, adoption allowances will be very important. With so many adopters in paid employment, paid adoption leave would surely make it possible for more adopters to come forward, particularly single parents.

It seemed surprising that adopters seem to have had younger children placed with them than they were prepared to adopt when they originally came forward. Nearly three-quarters of the adoptive parents who were prepared to accept a child aged up to four years had a younger child placed with them. This continued throughout the age bands with many more adopters approved for older children adopting younger children. Again, this indicates that further research is required as to whether adopters approved for older children are shared nationally when older children are not available locally, or whether this reflects the high proportion of children with adoption plans in the youngest age groups.

Sixty-two per cent of adopters who expressed a gender preference for their adopted child preferred to adopt a girl – although many of these adopters subsequently adopted boys. This gender issue is also reflected in BAAF's experience of far higher number of enquiries resulting in response to girls (BAAF, 2000). Further thought needs to be given to the social factors which currently discourage adopters of boys and how they might be addressed in recruitment campaigns.

The information in the study about the presence or not of other children in the adoptive family at the time of placement is again consistent with BAAF's previous study (Dance, 1997) with 71 per cent of all adopters having no birth children, including step-children. The fact that a quarter of all the adopters had already adopted a child must indicate that the creation of a family through adoption continues to be achieved through the adoption of children from care. This is in spite of the decline in the availability of relinquished infants for adoption which, in the past, had been the traditional route by which childless couples created a family. Adoption must have been a positive experience in order for families to wish to adopt more children. It was surprising that almost every child adopted in this study was the youngest child in the new family. While research evidence demonstrates placements are less likely to disrupt if a child is not too close in age to a child already living with the adoptive family, it is certainly not essential that every adopted child is the youngest in the family. This appears to be an aspect of custom and practice, which should be challenged if families are to be found for the wide range of children currently seeking adoption where a more flexible response to the age and presence of resident siblings may be required.

Adoption allowances

Since 1976, it has been possible to pay allowances to adopters to enable them to assume responsibility for children who would otherwise be "hard to place". Initially, agencies set up their own schemes for these allowances, subject to the approval of the Secretary of State. Since 1991, the schemes have been replaced by a regulatory framework. The survey data provide only very limited information on whether allowances were expected to be paid in a number of cases, and none whatsoever on the amount of any allowance or the circumstances on which decisions were based. What is clear is that 40 per cent of children had special needs (capable under the current regulations of establishing the threshold for payment of an allowance. In addition the need to keep siblings together, or to enable a child to maintain an existing relationship – eg, adoption by a child's foster carers – constitute grounds for the possible award of an allowance).

Interagency Placements

This study provides for the first time information about the numbers of children placed on an interagency basis. The larger shire authorities were able to place almost all their children from within their own resources whereas with only 12 per cent placed through other agencies, whereas 44 per cent of Inner London children were placed with families recruited elsewhere. Voluntary adoption agencies played a particularly important role in finding families for more children with complex needs including black and mixed parentage children and sibling groups. This confirms earlier studies (Dance, 1997) which found that a high proportion of children from these groups were placed through voluntary agencies. It is not known at what stage in the search for an appropriate placement an inter-agency placement was sought, but there would appear to be advantages for agencies considering these at an earlier stage if delay is to be minimised. One of the concerns expressed about using a National Register has been that children will be separated from their communities; it is therefore relevant to note that for 44 per cent of children, a decision had been reached that there should not be a local placement.

Conclusion

This is a rich and interesting study. In this chapter, I have endeavoured to draw attention to some of the findings, which will be of interest to policy makers, managers and practitioners – there are many more. The value of such statistical research is that it gives the opportunity for questions to be raised both about practice and also some of the populist rhetoric around adoption issues. It helps us to understand the reality of adoption today.

Thanks to Deborah Cullen and the Steering Group for their assistance in identifying key messages.

References

BAAF (2000) *Linking Children with Adoptive Parents*, London: BAAF.

Children Act Advisory Committee Report 1994/5, Lord Chancellor's Department.

Dance, C (1997) *Focus on Adoption: A snapshot of adoption patterns*, London: BAAF.

Department of Health (1998) *Adoption: achieving the right balance, LAC(98) 20*, London: Department of Health.

Handbook of Best Practice in Children Act Cases, June 1997.

Ivaldi, G (1998) *Children Adopted from Care: An examination of agency adoptions in England – 1996*, London: BAAF.

Ivaldi, G (2000) *Children and families in the Voluntary Sector: An overview of child placement and adoption work by the voluntary adoption agencies in England 1994–98*, London: BAAF.

PIU Report (2000) *Prime Minister's Review of Adoption*, London: The Cabinet Office